ALSACE TRAVELS

ALSACE TRAVEL GUIDE 2023

By James Bartlett

ALSACE TRAVELS

All rights reserved. No part of this publication may be reproduced, distributed, or transmitted in any form in any way from or by any means, including photocopying, recording, or other electronic or mechanical methods, without prior written permission of the publisher, except in the case of brief quotations embodied in critical reviews and certain other noncommercial uses permitted by copyright laws.

Copyright © James Bartlett, 2023

ALSACE TRAVELS

Table of Content

Introduction
Getting to Know Alsace
    1.1: Geography & Location
    1.2: History & Culture
    1.3: Climate & Weather
    1.4: Getting to Alsace
    1.5: Visa & Entry Requirements
Exploring Strasbourg
    2.1: Overview of Strasbourg
    2.2: Strasbourg Cathedral
    2.3: Petite France District
    2.4: European Parliament
    2.5: Museums in Strasbourg
    2.6: Boat Tours on the Ill River
    2.7: Parks & Gardens
Colmar & the Wine Route
    3.1: Colmar City Guide
    3.2: Unterlinden Museum
    3.3: The Little Venice District
    3.4: Wine Tasting in Alsace
    3.5: The Enchantment of Riquewihr Village
    3.6: Eguisheim Village; An Enchanting Wine Wonderland
    3.7: Kaysersberg Village; A Wine Lover's Paradise
Mulhouse & the Industrial Heritage

ALSACE TRAVELS

- 4.1: Mulhouse City Guide
- 4.2: Cité de l'Automobile
- 4.3: Cité du Train - A Window into the World of Trains
- 4.4: Mulhouse Zoological & Botanical Park - Nature's Haven
- 4.5: Other Museums in Mulhouse
- 4.6: Parc de la Citadelle

The Vosges Mountains
- 5.1: Overview
- 5.2: Hiking & Nature Trails
- 5.3: Ski Resorts in Alsace
- 5.4: Lac Blanc & Lac des Truites
- 5.5: Grand Ballon d'Alsace

Alsace Cuisine & Gastronomy
- 6.1: Traditional Alsatian Dishes
- 6.2: Wine & Wineries
- 6.3: Beer & Breweries in Alsace
- 6.4: Alsatian Cheeses
- 6.5: Food Festivals & Markets
- 6.6: Culinary Workshops

Off the Beaten Path
- 7.1: Offbeat Destinations in Alsace
- 7.2: Haut-Koenigsbourg Castle
- 7.3: Mont Sainte-Odile
- 7.4: Struthof Concentration Camp
- 7.5: Rhine River

Practical Information
- 8.1: Language, Communication & Useful Phrases
- 8.2: Currency & Banking
- 8.3: Transportation in Alsace
- 8.4: Accommodation Options

ALSACE TRAVELS

    8.5: Health, Safety & Emergency Contacts
    8.6: Local Customs & Etiquette
Festivals & Events
    9.1: Colmar International Festival
    9.2: Fête de la Bière
    9.3: Traditional Alsatian Celebrations
Travel Tips & Recommendations
    10.1: Best Time to Visit Alsace
    10.2: Packing Essentials
    10.3: Money-Saving Tips
    10.4: Itinerary
    10.5: Shopping in Alsace
    10.6: Traveling with Children & Pet
Conclusion
    11.1: Useful Mobile Apps
    11.2: Online Travel Resources
    11.3: Tourist Information Centers
    11.4: Final Thoughts

ALSACE TRAVELS

Introduction

"I embarked on my first trip to the captivating region of Alsace with great anticipation. Nestled in northeastern France, this picturesque land promised a tapestry of rich history, stunning landscapes, and delectable cuisine. Little did I know that this expedition would leave an indelible mark on my soul.

My adventure began in the enchanting city of Strasbourg, known for its medieval architecture and the iconic Notre-Dame Cathedral. The intricate carvings and awe-inspiring stained glass windows transported me to another era. A boat ride along the Ill River revealed the city's charming half-timbered houses and flower-laden bridges, a testament to its timeless beauty.

ALSACE TRAVELS

Leaving the city behind, I ventured into the countryside, where rolling vineyards stretched as far as the eye could see. The Alsace Wine Route beckoned, promising a sensory delight. Visiting family-owned wineries, I sampled their exquisite Rieslings and Gewürztraminers, understanding why Alsace is renowned for its world-class wines. The warm hospitality of the winemakers added a personal touch to this intoxicating experience.

As I ventured deeper into the heart of Alsace, the allure of its storybook villages unfolded before me. Eguisheim, with its concentric circles of colorful houses and cobbled streets, epitomized charm. Each corner seemed to reveal a hidden treasure, whether it be a flower-filled courtyard or a quaint café offering Alsatian specialties.

Obernai, with its medieval walls and charming squares, enchanted me with its timeless ambiance. Exploring its winding alleyways, I stumbled upon the birthplace of Sainte Odile, the patron saint of Alsace, and marveled at the views from Mont Sainte-Odile, where a thousand-year-old monastery nestled amidst serene forests.

The fairytale village of Riquewihr stole my heart with its perfectly preserved medieval architecture. The vibrant facades of the half-timbered houses housed quaint shops offering delicate porcelain and regional delicacies. The air was infused with the scent of freshly baked Kougelhopf, a traditional Alsatian cake, enticing me to indulge.

My Alsace journey would not have been complete without a visit to the historic town of Colmar. Its well-preserved old town, known as "Little Venice," delighted me with its charming canals and colorful buildings reflected in the water. The Unterlinden Museum, with its renowned

Isenheim Altarpiece, showcased the region's artistic legacy.

Every meal in Alsace felt like a celebration of flavors. From flammekueche, a savory Alsatian pizza topped with onions, bacon, and crème fraîche, to choucroute garnie, a hearty dish of sauerkraut and various types of meat, each bite was a revelation. The fusion of French and German culinary traditions created a unique and tantalizing gastronomic experience.

As I reluctantly bid farewell to Alsace, I carried with me memories of enchanting landscapes, captivating history, and warm-hearted people. This first-hand encounter with the region's charms left an indelible mark on my soul. From the fairy tale villages to the exquisite wines and delectable cuisine, Alsace had surpassed all my expectations. It is a place that demands to be explored, savored, and cherished, a true gem in the heart of Europe".

ALSACE TRAVELS

Welcome to Alsace, a captivating region nestled in the northeastern corner of France. Known for its rich history, charming villages, world-renowned wines, and stunning landscapes, Alsace offers a truly unique experience for travelers seeking to immerse themselves in the beauty and diversity of this enchanting destination. In this comprehensive guide, we will take you on a journey through the captivating geography, unique culture, and exceptional attractions that make Alsace a must-visit region.

ALSACE TRAVELS

Getting to Know Alsace

1.1: Geography & Location

Nestled in the northeastern corner of France, Alsace is a destination that beckons travelers with its timeless charm and picturesque vistas. Embark on a journey through this enchanting land and unlock the secrets of its geography and location.

Geography

Alsace is located in the Grand Est region of France, bordered by the Vosges Mountains to the west and the Rhine River to the east. This unique positioning has endowed Alsace with a diverse topography, where lush green plains meet rolling hills and majestic peaks. The region spans approximately 8,280 square kilometers and is divided into two departments: Bas-Rhin and Haut-Rhin.

Strasbourg, the capital of Alsace, is situated at the heart of the region and is known for its exceptional beauty. The city is straddled by the Ill River, which gracefully winds through its historic center. Strasbourg's distinctive blend of French and German influences can be traced back to its strategic location on the Rhine River, making it a melting pot of cultures and traditions.

Location

Alsace enjoys a strategic location at the crossroads of Europe, making it easily accessible from neighboring countries such as Germany and Switzerland. Its proximity to major transportation hubs, including the Strasbourg International Airport and the high-speed train network, allows for convenient travel connections, making

Alsace an ideal base for exploring the wider region.

Key Cities & Towns

Beyond Strasbourg, Alsace boasts a plethora of charming cities and towns, each offering its unique allure. Colmar, often referred to as the "Little Venice" of Alsace, enchants visitors with its colorful half-timbered houses and picturesque canals. The city's well-preserved medieval old town invites strolls and is a haven for art enthusiasts, housing the renowned Unterlinden Museum.

Mulhouse, known for its industrial heritage, surprises visitors with its vibrant energy and remarkable museums. The Cité de l'Automobile, the largest automobile museum in the world, showcases a stunning collection of vintage cars, while the Cité du Train takes you on a captivating journey through the history of rail transport.

Riquewihr and Eguisheim, two fairytale-like villages, epitomize the charm of Alsace with their cobblestone streets, flower-decked facades, and quaint atmosphere. These picturesque gems offer a glimpse into the region's rich architectural heritage and provide a tranquil respite amidst the rolling vineyards.

Natural Splendors

Nature lovers will be captivated by the stunning landscapes that grace the Alsace region. The Vosges Mountains, with their verdant forests and serene lakes, offer endless opportunities for outdoor activities. Hiking enthusiasts can conquer the peaks of the Vosges and savor panoramic views, while cyclists can meander through scenic routes that traverse the mountains.

The Wine Route, a scenic journey spanning over 170 kilometers, is a must-visit for oenophiles and those seeking bucolic charm. The route meanders through picturesque vineyards, dotted with wine-producing villages, where visitors can indulge in tastings of the world-renowned Alsace wines. From crisp Rieslings to aromatic Gewürztraminers, the region's wine heritage is as diverse as its landscape.

1.2: History & Culture

In this enchanting corner of the world, you will discover a unique blend of German and French influences, evident in architecture, cuisine, and traditions. Embark on a journey through time as we explore the rich tapestry of Alsace's history and delve into its vibrant cultural heritage.

The Ancient Origins

Our journey begins in prehistoric times when Alsace was inhabited by Celtic tribes.

The Romans later conquered the region and established thriving settlements, leaving behind a legacy of grandiose architecture and an intricate road network. Traces of this Roman influence can still be found in towns like Strasbourg, where the Romanesque cathedral stands tall as a testament to the past.

A Medieval Melting Pot

The medieval period witnessed a remarkable blending of cultures in Alsace. Throughout this era, the region became a crossroads between the Germanic and Romanic worlds, shaping its unique identity. The Alsatian towns flourished as prosperous trade centers, benefiting from the strategic location along the Rhine River. Strasbourg, Colmar, and Mulhouse emerged as prominent cities, boasting impressive medieval architecture that still enchants visitors today.

The Thirty Years' War & French Annexation

The seventeenth century brought upheaval to Alsace as it became a battleground during the devastating Thirty Years' War. The conflict ravaged the region, leaving it in ruins and causing widespread suffering. Eventually, Alsace fell under French control in 1681, marking the beginning of a new chapter in its history.

A Germanic Interlude

The Franco-Prussian War of 1870-1871 led to Alsace's brief return to German rule. The region thrived under German influence, with significant investments in infrastructure and education. The architecture adopted a distinctly Germanic style, visible in the half-timbered houses that dot the picturesque Alsatian villages. However, the Alsatians never fully embraced their German identity and continued to cherish their distinct Alsatian culture.

The World Wars & Reconciliation

The twentieth century brought immense suffering to Alsace during the two World Wars. The region suffered extensive damage, and its people endured the hardships of occupation. Alsace experienced a tumultuous tug-of-war between German and French influences, with its residents caught in the crossfire. However, after World War II, a spirit of reconciliation prevailed, and Alsace once again became an integral part of France.

Culture & Traditions

Alsatian culture is a captivating blend of German and French customs, creating a unique tapestry of traditions. The Alsatian dialect, a blend of German and French, is still spoken by some locals, preserving the linguistic heritage of the region. Folklore plays a significant role in Alsatian culture, with festivals like the Carnaval de Mulhouse and the Fête de l'Oignon celebrating the region's rich traditions.

Architecture & Art

The architecture of Alsace is a sight to behold, with timber-framed houses adorned with colorful flower boxes, ornate facades, and steep roofs. The picturesque village of Eguisheim, known for its concentric streets, is a prime example of Alsatian charm. The region also boasts impressive Gothic cathedrals, such as the Strasbourg Cathedral, a masterpiece of intricate stonework and stunning stained glass.

Gastronomy

A visit to Alsace would be incomplete without indulging in its world-renowned cuisine. Influenced by both German and

French culinary traditions, Alsatian dishes are a delightful fusion of flavors. The region is famous for its hearty dishes like choucroute (sauerkraut with sausages), baeckeoffe (meat and potato casserole), and flammekueche (thin savory tart). Pair these culinary delights with a glass of Alsatian wine, such as Riesling or Gewürztraminer, to truly savor the local gastronomic experience.

The Route des Vins

Wine enthusiasts will be delighted by the famous Route des Vins (Wine Route), winding through picturesque vineyards and charming villages. This scenic journey offers the opportunity to explore family-owned wineries, sample exquisite wines, and learn about the art of winemaking. From Riquewihr to Obernai, each village along the route exudes its distinct charm and showcases the rich winemaking heritage of the region.

Festivals & Celebrations

Throughout the year, Alsace comes alive with vibrant festivals and celebrations that reflect its deep-rooted traditions. The Christmas markets of Strasbourg and Colmar are renowned worldwide for their enchanting atmosphere, where twinkling lights, gingerbread treats, and handcrafted decorations evoke the magic of the holiday season. The Alsace Wine Fair in Colmar and the Fête de la Musique in Strasbourg are just a few of the many events that showcase the region's cultural vibrancy.

As you explore Alsace, be prepared to immerse yourself in a captivating blend of history and culture. From its ancient Roman roots to its medieval charm, from its turbulent past to its spirit of reconciliation, Alsace offers a unique experience that will leave an indelible mark on your soul. Discover the architectural wonders, relish the tantalizing cuisine, and embrace the warmth of the Alsatian people. In Alsace, the past and present intertwine, creating a cultural mosaic that is truly one-of-a-kind.

1.3: Climate & Weather

Situated between the Vosges Mountains and the Rhine River, Alsace experiences a unique climate influenced by both continental and oceanic factors. The region is known for its distinct seasonal variations, each offering its charm to visitors.

Spring

Spring in Alsace is a delightful season, with nature bursting into bloom. Temperatures gradually rise from March to May, ranging between 10°C (50°F) and 20°C (68°F). Showers are frequent but not excessive, bringing renewed freshness to the region. It is the perfect time to witness the colorful blossoms and vibrant vineyards that adorn the landscape.

Summer

Summer in Alsace is warm and sunny, creating an idyllic setting for outdoor exploration. From June to August, temperatures range from 20°C (68°F) to 30°C (86°F), occasionally reaching higher levels. Days are long and pleasant, providing ample opportunities to indulge in hiking, cycling, and exploring the charming towns and villages scattered across the region.

Autumn

Autumn in Alsace is a painter's palette of breathtaking hues. From September to November, temperatures gradually cool, ranging from 10°C (50°F) to 20°C (68°F). The region transforms into a mesmerizing tapestry of red, orange, and gold as vineyards and forests prepare for the harvest season. It's an excellent time to savor the local cuisine and witness the grape harvest festivities that epitomize the Alsace way of life.

Winter

Winter in Alsace casts a magical spell, turning the region into a winter wonderland. From December to February, temperatures range from -5°C (23°F) to 5°C (41°F), with occasional snowfall blanketing the landscape. The charming towns adorned with twinkling lights and the enticing aroma of mulled wine wafting through the air create an enchanting atmosphere. Winter sports enthusiasts can also enjoy skiing in the nearby Vosges Mountains.

1.4: Getting to Alsace

Now that we have acquainted ourselves with Alsace's climate, let's explore the various travel options available to reach this captivating region.

By Air

The primary airport serving Alsace is Strasbourg Airport (SXB), conveniently located near the capital city. It offers domestic and international flights, connecting Alsace to major European cities. Another nearby option is EuroAirport Basel-Mulhouse-Freiburg (BSL/MLH/EAP), situated on the French-Swiss border. From the airports, you can easily reach your desired destination in Alsace using public transportation, rental cars, or taxis.

By Train

Alsace benefits from an extensive rail network, making train travel a convenient option. The TGV (high-speed train) connects major French cities to Strasbourg, the region's main transportation hub. The journey from Paris to Strasbourg takes approximately two hours. Additionally, regional trains provide connections to smaller towns and villages within Alsace. The train stations are well-connected to public transportation, making it easy to reach your final destination.

By Car

If you prefer the freedom and flexibility of driving, reaching Alsace by car is a viable option. The region is well-served by a network of highways, including the A4 and A35, which provide access from neighboring countries such as Germany and Switzerland. The road infrastructure is excellent, and scenic routes offer breathtaking views of the countryside. Car rentals are available at major airports and train stations, allowing you to explore Alsace at your own pace.

By Bus

ALSACE TRAVELS

For budget-conscious travelers, buses offer an affordable means of reaching Alsace. Several bus companies operate routes connecting Alsace to nearby cities and countries. Eurolines and FlixBus are two prominent providers that offer comfortable and cost-effective travel options. Bus terminals are conveniently located in major cities, and local buses provide transportation within Alsace's towns and villages.

From the mesmerizing climate and seasonal beauty to the diverse travel options, Alsace promises an enchanting experience for every traveler.

1.5: Visa & Entry Requirements

Whether you're planning a short visit or a long-term stay, read on to discover all you need to know about visas, entry regulations, and essential documents for your trip to Alsace.

Visa Requirements

When it comes to visa requirements for visiting Alsace, it primarily depends on your nationality and the purpose and duration of your stay. The following information outlines the visa policies based on different scenarios:

- A. Schengen Agreement: Alsace, like the rest of France, is part of the Schengen Area. Citizens of Schengen member countries, including the European Union (EU) and the European Free Trade Association (EFTA), can enter Alsace without a visa for up to 90 days within 180 days. This rule applies to both tourist and business visits.

- B. Non-Schengen Countries: If you hold a passport from a non-Schengen country, you may require a visa to visit Alsace. The French authorities handle visa applications on behalf of Alsace. It is advisable to contact the nearest French embassy or consulate in your home country to determine the specific visa requirements, processing times, and necessary documentation.

C. Long-Term Stays: If you plan to stay in Alsace for longer than 90 days, you will need to apply for a long-stay visa. This type of visa grants you the right to reside in Alsace for an extended period. Long-stay visas are subject to specific requirements, such as employment, study, family reunification, or investment purposes. It is vital to consult the French embassy or consulate well in advance to gather accurate information and ensure a smooth application process.

Essential Documents

To ensure a hassle-free entry into Alsace, it is crucial to have the necessary documents readily available. Here is a checklist of essential documents you should prepare:

A. Valid Passport: All travelers visiting Alsace must possess a valid passport. Ensure that your passport has a validity of at least three months beyond the intended period of stay. It is advisable to check your passport's expiration date and renew it if necessary before your trip.

B. Visa: If your nationality requires a visa, you must obtain it before traveling to Alsace. Submit your visa application well in advance, providing all the required documents and paying the necessary fees. Remember to carry your visa with you during your trip.

C. Travel Insurance: While not a mandatory requirement, it is highly recommended to have travel insurance that covers medical emergencies, trip cancellation, and loss of personal belongings. In case of any unforeseen circumstances, travel insurance ensures you are adequately protected and can access necessary assistance.

D. Accommodation Details: It is advisable to have your accommodation details readily available upon arrival in Alsace. This includes hotel reservations, addresses of friends or family you may be staying with, or any other proof of accommodation you have arranged.

E. Return or Onward Ticket: Immigration authorities may request proof of onward travel, such as a return or onward ticket, to ensure you do not overstay your permitted duration. Carry a printed or digital copy of your travel itinerary or ticket to show your intention to leave Alsace within the allowed timeframe.

F. Financial Means: It is essential to demonstrate that you have sufficient financial means to support yourself during your stay in Alsace. Carry evidence such as bank statements, credit cards, or traveler's cheques to show your ability to cover accommodation, transportation, and daily expenses.

G. Purpose of Visit: If you are visiting Alsace for a specific purpose, such as attending a conference, business meetings, or educational programs, carry the necessary documentation to support your reason for travel. This may include invitation letters, event registrations, or acceptance letters from educational institutions.

H. Vaccination Certificates: While not currently mandatory, it is always a good idea to carry your vaccination certificates, especially in light of public health concerns. Stay informed about any specific vaccination requirements or recommendations by checking the website of the French Ministry of Health or consulting your healthcare provider.

I. Driving License: If you plan to rent a car and drive in Alsace, ensure that you have a valid driving license. Most countries' driving licenses are recognized in France, but it is recommended to carry an International Driving Permit (IDP) as an additional form of identification and to ease any language barriers during interactions with authorities.

Remember to keep all your documents organized, easily accessible, and protected during your journey. It is recommended to have both physical copies and digital backups to ensure their availability in case of loss or theft.

Entry Regulations

When arriving in Alsace, you will go through immigration and customs procedures. Understanding the entry regulations will help you navigate this process smoothly. In particular, remember the following:

> A. Border Control: Alsace shares borders with Germany and Switzerland, both Schengen member countries. If you are entering Alsace from another Schengen country, there are generally no immigration checks. However, it is advisable to carry your passport and other identification documents in case

of random checks or other exceptional circumstances.

B. Customs Regulations: France, including Alsace, has strict customs regulations regarding the importation of certain goods. It is important to be aware of the items that are prohibited or restricted, such as weapons, drugs, counterfeit goods, or endangered species products. Familiarize yourself with the customs regulations to avoid any legal issues or confiscation of goods.

C. Health Screening: In light of public health concerns, you may be subject to health screenings upon arrival in Alsace. This can include temperature checks, completion of health declaration forms, or providing proof of vaccination or negative COVID-19 test results. Stay updated with the latest health guidelines and requirements from the French Ministry of Health or relevant authorities.

D. Security Measures: As with any international travel, security measures are in place to ensure the safety of all passengers. These measures may include baggage checks, body scanners, or random security screenings. Cooperate with security personnel and follow their instructions for a smooth and efficient process.

Remember to check with the nearest French embassy or consulate regarding your specific nationality and circumstances, as requirements may vary.

As you immerse yourself in the breathtaking beauty, rich history, and warm hospitality of Alsace, ensure that you have all the necessary documentation prepared and readily accessible. By doing so, you can focus on creating lasting memories and exploring the wonders of this captivating region. Bon voyage and have a fantastic time in Alsace!

ALSACE TRAVELS

Exploring Strasbourg

Welcome to Strasbourg, a city that seamlessly combines history, culture, and natural beauty. Nestled in the heart of Europe, this enchanting city offers a captivating blend of French and German influences, resulting in a unique and vibrant atmosphere. In this guide, we will take you on a journey through the highlights of Strasbourg,Let's dive in!

2.1: Overview of Strasbourg

Situated in northeastern France, near the border with Germany, Strasbourg is the capital of the Alsace region and the official seat of several European institutions. With its rich history spanning over 2,000 years, the city showcases a fascinating fusion of architectural styles, cultural traditions, and culinary delights.

The historic city center, Grande Île, is a UNESCO World Heritage site and a true testament to Strasbourg's past. Its charming cobblestone streets, timber-framed houses, and picturesque canals create a romantic ambiance that is truly captivating. Strasbourg is renowned for having Christmas markets that draw tourists from all over the world.

The city boasts a diverse and multicultural population, and its unique blend of French and German cultures is reflected in its cuisine, language, and way of life. Strasbourg is a melting pot of flavors, offering a wide range of culinary experiences, from hearty Alsatian specialties to international delicacies.

Strasbourg's strategic location on the Rhine River has made it a vital hub for commerce and trade throughout history. Today, it is a thriving economic center and a symbol of European unity as the headquarters of the European Parliament and the European Court of Human Rights.

2.2: Strasbourg Cathedral

No visit to Strasbourg is complete without a visit to the magnificent Strasbourg Cathedral, known as Cathédrale Notre-Dame de Strasbourg. This architectural masterpiece is one of the finest examples of Gothic architecture in Europe and dominates the city skyline with its imposing presence.

The construction of the cathedral began in 1015 and took over 400 years to complete. Standing at a height of 142 meters, its spire was the tallest building in the world until the 19th century. The intricately carved façade, adorned with statues and ornamental details, is a true marvel to behold.

Step inside and be prepared to be awestruck by the soaring vaulted ceilings, the delicate stained glass windows, and the elaborate sculptures. The cathedral's astronomical clock, an engineering marvel of the Renaissance period, is a must-see. Don't miss the opportunity to climb to the top of the tower for breathtaking panoramic views of the city.

The cathedral also houses a remarkable collection of medieval and Renaissance art, including the famous "The Virgin and Child" by Hans Baldung. Whether you are an art enthusiast or a history buff, the Strasbourg Cathedral offers a truly immersive experience.

2.3: Petite France District

Nestled on the banks of the Ill River, the Petite France district is the epitome of charm and beauty. This picturesque neighborhood, with its half-timbered houses, winding canals, and flower-lined streets, is a postcard-perfect destination.

Originally a tanners' district, Petite France has retained its medieval character and exudes a romantic ambiance that is hard to resist. Take a stroll along the canals, cross the charming bridges, and immerse yourself in the enchanting atmosphere.

The district is home to several notable landmarks, such as the Maison des Tanneurs (Tanners' House), a beautifully preserved building that provides a glimpse into Strasbourg's industrial past. Nearby, the Ponts Couverts (Covered Bridges), a series of fortified bridges, add to the district's allure.

Exploring Petite France is a treat for the senses, with its quaint shops, delightful cafés, and traditional Alsatian restaurants. Indulge in the local cuisine, savoring dishes such as choucroute garnie (sauerkraut with sausages and meats) and flammekueche (thin crust pizza-like dish). Pair your meal with a glass of Alsatian wine for a truly authentic experience.

As you wander through the streets, you will encounter the Maison Kammerzell, a magnificent Renaissance building adorned with intricately carved woodwork and vibrant frescoes. This architectural gem now serves as a restaurant and offers a delightful setting to enjoy a meal or a drink.

For a unique perspective of Petite France, take a boat tour along the canals. Drift beneath the charming bridges, admire the colorful facades, and listen to the tales of the city's history from knowledgeable guides.

Strasbourg is a city that will captivate your heart and leave you with memories to cherish. From the awe-inspiring Strasbourg Cathedral to the idyllic Petite France district, this city is a true treasure trove of history, culture, and beauty.

2.4: European Parliament

Nestled in the heart of Strasbourg lies the European Parliament, a symbol of unity and collaboration among European nations. As the legislative branch of the European Union, the Parliament plays a crucial role in shaping the policies and laws that impact millions of people across Europe. Visitors have the unique opportunity to witness this influential institution in action, gaining valuable insight into the inner workings of European politics.

Visiting the European Parliament

To fully appreciate the European Parliament, it is recommended to participate in one of the guided tours available to the public. These tours offer a fascinating glimpse into the daily operations of the institution, as well as its historical and political significance. Experienced guides will lead you through the striking architecture and vast halls, shedding light on the Parliament's functions and the decision-making processes within.

The Architecture

The European Parliament building itself is a masterpiece of contemporary architecture. Designed by renowned French architect Architecture-Studio, the structure embodies the ideals of transparency and openness. The sleek glass facade symbolizes the accessibility of the Parliament to its citizens, while the distinctive tower, standing at 60 meters tall, acts as a beacon of democracy. Inside, the hemicycle, where parliamentary sessions take place, showcases a modern and functional design that fosters dialogue and collaboration.

The Hemicycle

The hemicycle is the focal point of the European Parliament, where debates and voting sessions occur. Designed in a semi-circle, it reflects the principles of equality and inclusivity, allowing each member state to have an equal voice. The seating arrangement follows a linguistic principle, with MEPs (Members of the European Parliament) grouped according to their language. Witnessing a session in progress is an immersive experience, as you observe representatives from various countries engaging in lively discussions on topics that shape the future of Europe.

Multimedia Exhibition & Visitor Center

To delve deeper into the European Parliament's history and functions, make sure to visit the multimedia exhibition and visitor center. Here, interactive displays, multimedia presentations, and informative exhibits offer a comprehensive understanding of the institution's evolution and its impact on European integration. Engaging with these resources provides visitors with valuable insights into the challenges and successes encountered along Europe's journey toward unity.

2.5: Museums in Strasbourg

Strasbourg's Cultural Tapestry

Strasbourg's museum scene is a treasure trove of history, art, and innovation. The city's rich and diverse heritage is brought to life through a collection of exceptional museums that cater to a wide range of interests. From ancient artifacts to contemporary art, Strasbourg's museums offer something for every curious traveler.

The Strasbourg Museum of Fine Arts

Located in a splendid 18th-century palace, the Strasbourg Museum of Fine Arts houses an impressive collection spanning several centuries. Visitors can marvel at masterpieces by renowned artists such as Botticelli, Rembrandt, and Monet, as well as explore the works of regional artists. The museum's carefully curated exhibitions showcase the evolution of artistic styles and movements, providing a captivating journey through the world of visual arts.

The Alsatian Museum

Embark on a cultural adventure at the Alsatian Museum, where the unique identity of the Alsace region comes to life. Housed in charming timber-framed buildings, this museum offers a glimpse into Alsatian history, traditions, and craftsmanship. Discover intricately furnished period rooms, and traditional costumes, and explore the Alsatian way of life through the ages. It's an opportunity to understand the rich cultural heritage that shapes the region's identity.

The Museum of Modern & Contemporary Art

For those with an affinity for modern and contemporary art, a visit to the Museum of Modern and Contemporary Art is a must. Housed in a striking glass building, this museum showcases an impressive collection of works by artists from the 19th century to the present day. From Picasso to Warhol, visitors can appreciate a diverse range of artistic expressions through paintings, sculptures, installations, and multimedia creations.

The Historical Museum of Strasbourg

Step back in time at the Historical Museum of Strasbourg, housed in several historic buildings, including the former slaughterhouse. This museum traces the city's history from its origins to the present day, offering a comprehensive overview of its cultural, social, and political development. Explore archaeological artifacts, and medieval treasures, and immerse yourself in the captivating stories that have shaped Strasbourg over the centuries.

The Tomi Ungerer Museum

Art enthusiasts, both young and old, will find delight in the Tomi Ungerer Museum. Dedicated to the renowned illustrator and author, this museum celebrates Ungerer's creative legacy. The collection includes a vast array of his illustrations, books, and sculptures, showcasing his unique blend of humor, satire, and social commentary. It's a whimsical and inspiring journey into the imaginative world of one of Strasbourg's most beloved artists.

Strasbourg's blend of European political importance and vibrant museum scene creates a captivating destination for travelers. The European Parliament offers a window into the workings of European politics, while the city's museums provide an opportunity to explore its rich history, art, and culture. From the architectural marvel of the European Parliament building to the masterpieces housed in the Museum of Fine Arts, Strasbourg offers a truly enriching experience. Immerse yourself in the dynamic atmosphere of this city, where the past and present intertwine to create a unique tapestry of European heritage.

2.6: Boat Tours on the Ill River

The Ill River

Flowing through the heart of Strasbourg, the Ill River is a lifeline that connects the city's most beautiful sights. Taking a boat tour along the Ill River is an ideal way to explore the city's historic quarters and enjoy breathtaking views of its iconic landmarks.

Batorama Boat Tours

Embark on a Batorama boat tour and discover the magic of Strasbourg from the water. These guided tours provide an excellent introduction to the city, allowing you to admire its architectural marvels, such as the Strasbourg Cathedral, Petite France, and the European Parliament. Knowledgeable guides share fascinating stories and insights about the city's history and culture, making your journey even more captivating.

L'Ochsenfeld Cruise

ALSACE TRAVELS

For a more personalized experience, consider a private cruise with L'Ochsenfeld. This intimate boat tour allows you to customize your itinerary, giving you the freedom to explore the Ill River at your own pace. Enjoy the tranquility of the water as you pass by beautiful bridges, half-timbered houses, and lush greenery. L'Ochsenfeld provides a unique perspective, allowing you to immerse yourself in the city's charm.

The Covered Bridges

As you cruise along the Ill River, you will encounter the enchanting covered bridges that add to the city's allure. The Ponts Couverts, with its medieval towers and fortified walls, is a remarkable sight to behold. These bridges were once crucial for the city's defense and are now an iconic symbol of Strasbourg.

Evening Boat Tours

For a romantic and atmospheric experience, embark on an evening boat tour. As dusk sets in, the city is bathed in a warm glow, creating a magical ambiance. The illuminated bridges, historic buildings, and charming streets take on a whole new level of beauty, offering a truly unforgettable experience.

2.7: Parks & Gardens

The Parc de l'Orangerie

A visit to Strasbourg is incomplete without exploring the Parc de l'Orangerie, one of the city's largest and most beautiful parks. Nestled between the European Parliament and the University, this verdant oasis provides a serene retreat from the bustling city center. Stroll along tree-lined paths, admire vibrant flower beds and relax by the picturesque lake. The park is also home to the Strasbourg Zoo, where you can encounter a diverse range of animal species.

Jardin des Deux Rives

For a cross-border experience, venture to the Jardin des Deux Rives, a unique park that stretches between Strasbourg, France, and Kehl, Germany. This expansive green space is an architectural marvel, featuring stunning contemporary designs and offering breathtaking views of both countries. Enjoy a leisurely walk or bike ride along the Rhine River, explore the charming gardens, and relish the harmonious blend of French and German influences.

The Botanical Gardens

Nature enthusiasts will be delighted by the Botanical Gardens, a true horticultural gem. Nestled within the University's campus, these gardens boast a remarkable collection of plant species from around the world.

Explore themed gardens, including medicinal plants, tropical greenhouses, and even a Japanese garden. The tranquil ambiance and the exquisite variety of flora make it a perfect spot for relaxation and rejuvenation.

Contades Garden

Situated near the European Quarter, the Contades Garden offers a peaceful escape in the heart of the city. Adorned with elegant statues, vibrant flower beds, and neatly trimmed hedges, this garden exudes timeless charm. Enjoy a leisurely picnic, read a book under the shade of trees, or simply soak in the tranquil atmosphere while marveling at the surrounding architectural wonders.

Heyritz Park

For a modern and urban green space experience, visit Heyritz Park. This contemporary park, located along the Canal du Faux Rempart, is a popular spot for locals and visitors alike. Explore the innovative playgrounds, enjoy a game of petanque, or simply relax on the inviting lawns. The park's unique design, blending nature and urban elements, offers a refreshing take on green spaces.

Strasbourg's boat tours on the Ill River and its captivating parks and gardens provide a harmonious balance between cultural exploration and serene natural beauty. Whether you choose to cruise along the Ill River, take in the city's iconic sights, or immerse yourself in the tranquility of its parks and gardens, The experience you have in Strasbourg will stick with you long after your trip. So, embark on this enchanting journey and discover the hidden treasures of this remarkable city.

Colmar & the Wine Route

Welcome to Colmar and the Wine Route, an enchanting region in the heart of Alsace, France. This comprehensive travel guide will take you on a captivating journey through the picturesque town of Colmar and its surrounding vineyards. Immerse yourself in the rich history, culture, and natural beauty of this remarkable destination. Whether you're a wine enthusiast, a history buff, or simply seeking a charming getaway, Colmar and the Wine Route offers an experience like no other.

3.1: Colmar City Guide

Nestled in the Alsace region, Colmar is a gem of medieval architecture and old-world charm. Here, you'll find cobblestone streets, half-timbered houses, and flower-decked canals, creating a fairytale atmosphere. Begin your exploration at the well-preserved Old Town, known as "La Petite Venise" (Little Venice) for its canals reminiscent of the Italian city. Stroll along the Quai de la Poissonnerie, where colorful buildings reflect in the water, creating a postcard-perfect scene.

Another must-visit site is the Collegiate Church of Saint-Martin, a striking Gothic masterpiece that dates back to the 14th century. Its impressive spire dominates the city's skyline and offers breathtaking views from the top. Nearby, the Dominican Church and its famous pink sandstone façade are equally worth a visit.

For art enthusiasts, the Musee d'Unterlinden is a treasure trove of artistic marvels. Let's explore this renowned museum further in the next section.

3.2: Unterlinden Museum

Located in a former 13th-century convent, the Unterlinden Museum houses an exceptional collection of art and artifacts spanning several centuries. The museum's centerpiece is the Isenheim Altarpiece, a masterpiece by Matthias Grünewald. This magnificent polyptych is considered one of the most significant works of religious art in the world. Its intricate details and emotional depth are truly awe-inspiring.

Beyond the Isenheim Altarpiece, the museum showcases a diverse range of art, from medieval sculptures to contemporary pieces. Explore the collection of Renaissance paintings, archaeological finds, and decorative arts. Don't miss the opportunity to admire the stunning architecture of the museum itself, which beautifully integrates both old and modern elements.

3.3: The Little Venice District

The charm of Colmar reaches its pinnacle in the Little Venice district. As you wander through its narrow streets, you'll encounter quaint houses adorned with colorful flowers, small cafés, and boutique shops. This area derives its name from the picturesque canals that wind their way through the district, evoking the ambiance of Venice.

Take a boat ride along the canals to fully immerse yourself in the enchanting atmosphere. Relax as you glide past centuries-old buildings and soak in the captivating scenery. You'll gain a unique perspective of Colmar's architecture and witness the town's beauty from a different angle.

Exploring the Wine Route

No visit to Colmar would be complete without embarking on a journey along the famous Alsace Wine Route. This scenic route stretches over 170 kilometers, weaving through vineyards, charming villages, and medieval castles. Immerse yourself in the region's winemaking traditions and sample some of the finest wines produced in France.

Begin your wine adventure by visiting the nearby village of Eguisheim, renowned for its well-preserved medieval architecture and vine-covered houses. Take a stroll through the narrow streets, admire the colorful facades, and visit local wineries for a taste of the region's delicious wines.

Continue your journey along the Wine Route, stopping at picturesque villages such as Riquewihr, Hunawihr, and Turckheim. These villages exude a timeless charm, with their half-timbered houses and flower-filled balconies. Explore local wineries, where passionate winemakers will share their knowledge and offer delightful wine tastings.

Beyond wine, the region offers numerous outdoor activities. Hike through the vineyards, cycle along the scenic paths, or simply savor a picnic amidst breathtaking landscapes. Each season paints the Wine Route with its unique colors, creating a captivating backdrop for your journey.

Colmar and the Wine Route provide a harmonious blend of history, culture, and natural beauty. From the fairytale-like streets of Colmar's Old Town to the world-renowned Unterlinden Museum, every corner of this region offers an unforgettable experience. Explore the enchanting canals of the Little Venice district and venture along the Wine Route to taste the exceptional wines that have made Alsace famous.

With its captivating scenery, rich heritage, and warm hospitality, Colmar and the Wine Route are sure to leave an indelible mark on your travel memories. Embrace the charm of this extraordinary destination and allow yourself to be swept away by its timeless allure. Plan your visit to Colmar and the Wine Route today, and embark on a journey you'll treasure forever.

3.4: Wine Tasting in Alsace

Wine Tasting Experiences

Alsace offers an array of wine-tasting experiences, catering to different preferences and budgets. From intimate tastings in family-owned wineries to guided tours in larger estates, there is something for everyone. Some wineries even provide food pairings to enhance the tasting experience, allowing visitors to savor the region's culinary delights alongside the wines.

Riesling, the Jewel of Alsace

Riesling, the flagship grape variety of Alsace, deserves special attention. Known for its elegance, purity, and exceptional aging potential, Alsace Riesling offers a range of styles, from bone-dry to lusciously sweet. Visit renowned Riesling producers such as Trimbach, Zind-Humbrecht, or Hugel & Fils to taste the epitome of this remarkable grape.

Gewürztraminer, the Aromatic Delight

Gewürztraminer, with its exotic aromas and spicy notes, is another gem of Alsace. This grape variety produces highly aromatic and full-bodied wines, often accompanied by flavors of lychee, rose petals, and tropical fruits. Plan a visit to Domaine Weinbach or Dopff au Moulin to indulge in the captivating flavors of Gewürztraminer.

Pinot Gris & Muscat

Hidden Treasures Pinot Gris, known as Tokay Pinot Gris until 2007, thrives in Alsace's favorable climate. It yields rich, textured wines with a delicate balance between fruitiness and acidity. Muscat, on the other hand, offers a captivating range of dry and sweet wines, expressing floral and fruity characteristics. Don't miss the opportunity to sample these hidden treasures at Domaine Zind Humbrecht or Domaine Marcel Deiss.

Wine Tasting Etiquette

When participating in wine tastings, it's essential to observe certain etiquettes to fully appreciate the experience. Remember to swirl, sniff, and sip the wine to evaluate its appearance, aromas, and flavors. Engage with the winemaker or sommelier, ask questions, and take notes to document your preferences. Additionally, be sure to taste

ALSACE TRAVELS

wines in moderation and make use of spittoons if necessary.

3.5: The Enchantment of Riquewihr Village

Nestled among vineyards and rolling hills, Riquewihr is a well-preserved medieval village that captivates visitors with its fairy-tale charm. Its distinctive half-timbered houses, narrow streets, and flower-filled balconies transport you to a bygone era. Riquewihr is also famous for its well-preserved fortifications and the Dolder Tower, offering panoramic views of the surrounding vineyards and the Vosges Mountains.

Exploring Riquewihr's Heritage

Take a stroll through Riquewihr's cobblestone streets, and you'll discover a treasure trove of historical sites and architectural wonders. The 16th-century Town Hall, with its remarkable façade, is a sight to behold. Don't miss Maison Schoenenbourg, a beautiful Renaissance house adorned with intricate sculptures. The 13th-century Thieves' Tower and the Sainte-Marguerite Church are also must-visit landmarks.

Wine & Gastronomy in Riquewihr

Riquewihr offers a diverse culinary scene that beautifully complements its wines. Indulge in the regional cuisine at traditional winstubs, where you can savor Alsatian specialties like choucroute garnie (sauerkraut with sausages and cured meats) or tarte flambée (thin, crispy pizza-like dish). Pair these delectable dishes with local wines for an unforgettable gastronomic experience.

Wine Festivals & Events

Throughout the year, Riquewihr hosts vibrant wine festivals and events that celebrate the region's viticultural heritage. The Riquewihr Wine Festival, held annually in July, is a lively affair where you can immerse yourself in the local culture, taste exceptional wines, and enjoy music and dance performances. Other notable events include the Riesling Festival and the Harvest Festival, offering unique insights into Alsace's wine traditions.

3.6: Eguisheim Village; An Enchanting Wine Wonderland

Nestled in the heart of the Alsace wine region, Eguisheim Village is a captivating destination for wine lovers. Its unique charm lies in its medieval architecture, cobblestone streets, and flower-filled alleyways. As you wander through this fairytale-like village, you'll find yourself surrounded by vineyards that stretch as far as the eye can see.

Historical Significance

Eguisheim boasts a rich winemaking history that dates back over a millennium. It was here that the famous Saint-Leon IX, a native of Eguisheim, played a crucial role in promoting viticulture during the Middle Ages. Today, the village pays homage to its heritage with traditional wine festivals and celebrations that showcase its deep-rooted connection to winemaking.

Vineyards & Terroir

Eguisheim's vineyards are renowned for producing exceptional wines, thanks to its unique terroir. The region's gentle slopes, composed of mineral-rich soil, coupled with an ideal microclimate, create the perfect conditions for grape cultivation. Riesling,

Gewürztraminer, Pinot Gris, and Muscat are some of the grape varieties that thrive in this terroir, resulting in wines that are renowned for their elegance and complexity.

Wine Tasting Experiences

Eguisheim offers a myriad of wine-tasting experiences that cater to all preferences. The village is home to numerous wineries and cellars, each with its distinctive character and expertise. From family-owned vineyards to larger, well-established wineries, you'll find a diverse range of options to explore.

During your visit, we recommend starting your wine journey at the Maison Martin Jund, a charming winery known for its dedication to organic winemaking practices. Here, you can partake in guided tours, where you'll learn about the winemaking process and sample their impressive selection of wines.

For a more immersive experience, visit Domaine Paul Blanck & Fils, a renowned winery that has been producing exceptional wines for generations. Delve into their cellar, where oak barrels age their wines to perfection, and delight your palate with their signature Grand Cru wines.

To truly immerse yourself in the wine culture of Eguisheim, don't miss the opportunity to participate in the annual Winegrowers' Festival. Held in late August, this vibrant event showcases the village's winemaking traditions, complete with colorful parades, wine tastings, and live entertainment.

Gastronomy & Local Delights

In Eguisheim, wine is not just a drink; it's an integral part of the local gastronomy. Indulge in the culinary delights that complement the region's wines, such as tarte flambée, a thin, crispy flatbread topped with cream, onions, and bacon. Pair this traditional dish with a glass of aromatic Gewürztraminer for a truly harmonious experience.

Immerse yourself in the local culture by visiting charming wine taverns, where you can savor regional delicacies, including escargots à l'alsacienne (Alsace-style snails) and choucroute garnie (sauerkraut with sausages and smoked meats). These dishes perfectly complement the wines of Eguisheim, allowing you to indulge in a symphony of flavors.

3.7: Kaysersberg Village; A Wine Lover's Paradise

Situated in the heart of the Alsatian vineyards, Kaysersberg Village is a postcard-perfect destination that will enchant wine enthusiasts and history buffs alike. With its medieval charm, stunning landscapes, and exceptional wines, Kaysersberg offers an unforgettable experience.

Historical Heritage

Kaysersberg is steeped in history, with a heritage that dates back to the 13th century. Stroll through the village's enchanting streets and admire its well-preserved half-timbered houses and the magnificent ruins of the Kaysersberg Castle. Discover the story of Albert Schweitzer, the Nobel Peace Prize laureate born in Kaysersberg, and explore the fascinating Alsatian traditions that have shaped the village's identity.

Vineyards & Wine Varieties

Kaysersberg is nestled amidst rolling vineyards that produce some of the finest wines in Alsace. The region benefits from a favorable terroir, characterized by granite and sandy soil, which imparts unique flavors and aromas to the grapes. Pinot Blanc, Pinot Gris, and Gewürztraminer are among the prominent grape varieties cultivated in Kaysersberg, resulting in wines that are full of character and finesse.

Wine Tasting Experiences

Embark on an unforgettable wine-tasting journey in Kaysersberg, where winemakers take great pride in their craft. Begin your exploration at the Domaine Weinbach, a prestigious winery known for its exceptional Riesling and Gewürztraminer wines. Take a guided tour of the vineyard and cellar, and indulge in a tasting session that will captivate your senses.

For a more intimate experience, visit Domaine Rolly-Gassmann, a family-owned winery with a history spanning over 400 years. Here, you'll have the opportunity to taste their diverse range of wines, including rare and unique varietals. The winery's charming ambiance and knowledgeable staff ensure a memorable visit.

Local Gastronomy & Culinary Delights

Kaysersberg is a haven for gastronomy enthusiasts, offering a plethora of culinary delights to accompany its exquisite wines. Sample traditional Alsatian dishes such as baeckeoffe, a hearty casserole of slow-cooked meats and potatoes, or fleischnacka, a dish of rolled pasta filled with meat and herbs. Pair these flavorsome dishes with a glass of Kaysersberg's famous Gewürztraminer for a culinary symphony.

Eguisheim and Kaysersberg Villages epitomize the magic of Alsace, where history, culture, and winemaking unite. The vineyards that blanket these villages produce wines that are revered worldwide, and the enchanting streets beckon travelers to immerse themselves in their beauty. Whether you're an avid wine connoisseur or simply seeking a unique travel experience, Eguisheim and Kaysersberg offer the perfect blend of wine tasting, cultural exploration, and natural splendor. Visit these charming villages, and allow the essence of Alsace to captivate your senses as you savor the finest wines and create lifelong memories. Cheers to an unforgettable journey!

Mulhouse & the Industrial Heritage

Welcome to Mulhouse, a city known for its rich industrial heritage and vibrant culture. Located in the eastern part of France,

ALSACE TRAVELS

Mulhouse is a fascinating destination that offers a unique blend of history, technology, and art. In this comprehensive city guide, we will take you on a journey through the highlights of Mulhouse, with a particular focus on the renowned Cité de l'Automobile. So grab your travel map, put on your walking shoes, and get ready to explore this captivating city.

4.1: Mulhouse City Guide

Mulhouse, also known as the "French Manchester," has a long-standing history as a major industrial center. The city flourished during the 19th and 20th centuries, thanks to its thriving textile and mechanical engineering industries. Today, Mulhouse is not only a testament to its industrial past but also a hub of innovation, art, and culture.

Getting to Mulhouse

Mulhouse is conveniently located in the Alsace region, close to the borders of Germany and Switzerland. The city is well-served by several different modes of transportation. If you're arriving by air, EuroAirport Basel-Mulhouse-Freiburg is the closest international airport. From there, you can easily reach Mulhouse by train or bus. The city also has excellent rail connections, making it accessible from major cities in France and Europe.

Exploring Mulhouse

Old Town (La Ville)

Start your journey in the heart of Mulhouse by visiting the picturesque Old Town. Wander through its narrow streets lined with charming half-timbered houses, cafes, and shops. Admire the stunning architecture of the 16th-century Town Hall (Hôtel de Ville) and the majestic Temple

Saint-Étienne, a beautiful Protestant church. Don't miss the opportunity to explore the bustling market square, Place de la Réunion, where you can sample local delicacies and soak up the vibrant atmosphere.

Mulhouse Historical Museum

Discover the city's fascinating history at the Mulhouse Historical Museum. Housed in the former city hall, this museum showcases the evolution of Mulhouse and its industries over the centuries. From textiles to automobiles, you'll find an impressive collection of artifacts, documents, and interactive displays that bring the past to life. It's a must-visit for history enthusiasts and anyone interested in the industrial heritage of Mulhouse.

Mulhouse Zoo

For a memorable family outing, head to the Mulhouse Zoo, one of the oldest zoos in France. Spanning over 25 hectares, this zoological park is home to a diverse range of animals from around the world. Wander through themed areas, such as the African Savannah or the South American Rainforest, and observe majestic lions, playful monkeys, and colorful birds up close. The Mulhouse Zoo is committed to conservation and education, making it an enriching experience for visitors of all ages.

Parc de l'Orangerie

Escape the hustle and bustle of the city at Parc de l'Orangerie, a peaceful oasis located near the city center. This beautifully landscaped park features manicured gardens, a serene lake, and charming pavilions. Take a stroll, have a picnic on the grass, or rent a rowboat to explore the tranquil waters. With its tranquil ambiance,

Parc de l'Orangerie offers the perfect respite from your urban adventures.

4.2: Cité de l'Automobile

Prepare to embark on a journey through automotive history at the Cité de l'Automobile. Located in an impressive former Schlumpf textile factory, this museum is the largest automobile collection in the world. It houses over 500 exceptional vehicles, including rare vintage cars, iconic models, and racing legends. Whether you're a car enthusiast or simply curious about the evolution of automobiles, the Cité de l'Automobile is an absolute must-visit.

Collections & Highlights

Step into the world of automotive marvels as you explore the diverse collections of the Cité de l'Automobile. Marvel at the elegance of early horseless carriages, such as the steam-powered De Dion Bouton et Trépardoux. Admire the engineering feats of the Bugatti collection, which features iconic models like the Bugatti Royale and the Bugatti Veyron. Explore the evolution of racing cars, from the legendary Mercedes-Benz Silver Arrows to the high-performance Formula 1 machines.

Schlumpf Collection

The crown jewel of the Cité de l'Automobile is undoubtedly the Schlumpf Collection. This extraordinary assembly of over 120 luxury cars showcases the passion and vision of the Schlumpf brothers, avid collectors, and industrialists. Marvel at the impeccable craftsmanship and timeless beauty of classic models from prestigious brands like Rolls-Royce, Bentley, and Hispano-Suiza. The Schlumpf Collection is a testament to the artistry and engineering prowess that has shaped the automotive industry.

Museography & Interactive Exhibits

The Cité de l'Automobile offers a captivating museum experience with its innovative museography and interactive exhibits. Immerse yourself in the world of automobile design and technology through interactive displays, virtual reality experiences, and multimedia presentations. Gain insights into the manufacturing process, the evolution of automotive design, and the social impact of cars on society. The museum's engaging approach ensures that visitors of all ages can appreciate the beauty and significance of the automobile.

Practical Information

Opening Hours & Admission

The Cité de l'Automobile is open daily, except for certain public holidays. Check the official website for the most up-to-date information on opening hours and special events. Admission fees vary depending on the type of ticket and age group. Students, older citizens, and families frequently qualify for discounts. It is recommended to allocate at least half a day to fully explore the museum and its collections.

Getting to the Cité de l'Automobile

The Cité de l'Automobile is located just outside the city center and can be easily reached by public transportation. Take tram line 2 or bus line 12 to the "Musée de l'Automobile" stop. If you prefer to drive, ample parking is available on-site. The museum is also accessible for visitors with disabilities, with ramps and elevators throughout the premises.

Mulhouse is a city that seamlessly blends its industrial past with a vibrant present. From the charming Old Town to the captivating Cité de l'Automobile, this city guide has highlighted some of the key attractions that make Mulhouse a unique destination for travelers. Immerse yourself in the history, culture, and innovation that define this remarkable city. Whether you're exploring the industrial heritage or indulging in the local cuisine, Mulhouse promises an unforgettable experience. So pack your bags, embark on an adventure, and discover the wonders of Mulhouse, the city where heritage and innovation collide.

4.3: Cité du Train - A Window into the World of Trains

The Cité du Train, located in Mulhouse, is a remarkable museum that chronicles the evolution of trains, their significance in shaping history, and their impact on society. With an unrivaled collection of over 100 locomotives, this expansive museum offers a comprehensive insight into the world of trains. Here, visitors can embark on an immersive journey through time and discover the marvels of rail transportation.

History Unveiled

Delve into the captivating history of trains as you wander through the extensive exhibition halls of the Cité du Train. From the humble beginnings of steam-powered locomotives to the revolutionary advances in technology, you'll witness the progression of train design and engineering over the centuries. Marvel at the meticulously restored locomotives, each with its own story to tell, and gain a deeper appreciation for the role trains played in transforming society.

Engaging Exhibits

The museum boasts a diverse range of interactive exhibits that cater to visitors of all ages. Step into the recreated train cabins and experience what it was like to be a passenger during different eras. Get a glimpse into the lives of train conductors and engineers through captivating displays and multimedia presentations. Immerse yourself in the sights and sounds of railway stations from various periods, allowing you to truly comprehend the historical context of train travel.

Discovering the Locomotive Legends

Prepare to be awestruck by the sheer scale and beauty of the locomotives on display at the Cité du Train. Marvel at iconic engines such as the world-famous Orient Express and the majestic TGV. Learn about the technological advancements that made these machines possible and how they revolutionized the transportation industry. Explore the intricacies of locomotive design, from the elegant aesthetics to the innovative engineering that powered these giants of the tracks.

Behind the Scenes

For those eager to gain deeper insights, the Cité du Train offers exclusive guided tours that take you behind the scenes. Accompanied by experts, you'll have the opportunity to explore the restoration workshops and witness firsthand the meticulous craftsmanship that goes into preserving these historical treasures. Gain a deeper understanding of the conservation efforts undertaken to maintain these locomotives for future generations to appreciate.

4.4: Mulhouse Zoological & Botanical Park - Nature's Haven

Immerse yourself in the breathtaking beauty of nature at the Mulhouse Zoological and Botanical Park. This sprawling sanctuary is home to an incredible array of wildlife, diverse ecosystems, and meticulously curated gardens, making it a haven for nature enthusiasts and animal lovers alike.

A Tapestry of Biodiversity

Embark on a journey of discovery as you wander through the park's diverse habitats, each carefully designed to replicate the natural environments of its inhabitants. Encounter majestic big cats, playful primates, and graceful birds as you traverse the well-maintained pathways. The park's commitment to conservation and education is evident, providing visitors with an opportunity to learn about the importance of protecting and preserving Earth's biodiversity.

Gardens of Serenity

Take a moment to soak in the tranquil beauty of the park's botanical gardens.

Wander through meticulously manicured landscapes, fragrant flower beds, and serene ponds, providing a welcome respite from the bustling city. Each section of the garden showcases a distinct theme, from exotic tropical flora to enchanting Japanese gardens, offering a harmonious blend of colors, scents, and textures.

Educational Experiences

The Mulhouse Zoological and Botanical Park goes beyond providing a visual spectacle; it also offers educational experiences for visitors of all ages. Engage in interactive presentations and animal feeding sessions led by knowledgeable guides, allowing you to learn more about the unique behaviors and conservation challenges faced by the park's inhabitants. These experiences foster a deeper appreciation for the importance of preserving and protecting endangered species.

Sustainable Initiatives

The park prides itself on its commitment to sustainability and eco-friendly practices. From renewable energy sources to waste reduction programs, the Mulhouse Zoological and Botanical Park demonstrates its dedication to minimizing its ecological footprint. By visiting this exceptional attraction, you are supporting their ongoing efforts to create a greener future for both animals and humans.

4.5: Other Museums in Mulhouse

Musée de l'Impression sur Étoffes

Immerse yourself in the enchanting world of textile art at the Musée de l'Impression sur Étoffes, a testament to Mulhouse's historical prominence in the textile industry. Housed in an elegant 19th-century mansion, this museum showcases the intricate art of fabric printing, tracing its origins back to the 18th century.

Marvel at the extensive collection of printed fabrics, ranging from delicate silks to vibrant cotton prints. Witness the evolution of textile techniques through the museum's exhibits, which feature ancient wooden printing blocks, machinery, and tools used in the production process. Discover the captivating stories of Mulhouse's textile trade and its impact on the global fashion industry.

Partake in hands-on workshops and demonstrations, where skilled artisans reveal the secrets of traditional textile printing techniques. Create your unique fabric masterpiece under their expert guidance, gaining a deeper appreciation for the craftsmanship that goes into each intricate design.

Musée de l'Électricité

Prepare to be amazed by the Musée de l'Électricité, an extraordinary museum dedicated to the exploration of electricity's wonders. Housed in an impressive power station building, this museum offers an enlightening experience of the history, science, and practical applications of electricity.

Embark on an immersive journey through interactive displays and captivating exhibits, illustrating the revolutionary discoveries and inventions that shaped the modern world. Uncover the contributions of renowned scientists, such as Nikola Tesla and Thomas Edison, and witness their groundbreaking experiments.

Explore the museum's diverse sections, including the "Energy Factory" and "Electro Expo," which provide insights into energy generation, transmission, and consumption. Engage with hands-on experiments, virtual reality simulations, and informative multimedia presentations, unraveling the mysteries of this vital force that powers our everyday lives.

Musée Historique de Mulhouse

Step back in time as we venture to the Musée Historique de Mulhouse, a treasure trove of historical artifacts and cultural heritage. Housed in a splendid Renaissance-style building, this museum narrates the compelling story of Mulhouse, from its medieval origins to its industrial prominence.

Discover an impressive collection of archaeological finds, religious art, traditional crafts, and historical documents that offer a glimpse into the city's past. Admire the meticulously restored rooms, adorned with period furniture, tapestries, and decorative arts, recreating the ambiance of bygone eras.

Explore thematic exhibitions that shed light on key aspects of Mulhouse's history, including its involvement in the textile trade, religious and social life, and the impact of industrialization. The museum also hosts temporary exhibitions, educational programs, and cultural events that further enrich the visitor experience.

EDF Electropolis Museum

Our final highlight, the EDF Electropolis Museum, offers a captivating exploration of the history and significance of electricity in society. Delve into the fascinating world of electrical engineering and its impact on our daily lives through this thought-provoking institution.

Discover the heritage of the French national electricity company, EDF, as you explore the museum's comprehensive exhibits. Trace the milestones of electrical development, from the early discoveries to the modern technologies that power our homes and industries.

Engage with interactive displays, engaging experiments, and engaging multimedia presentations that illustrate the principles of electricity. Marvel at vintage electrical appliances, early electrical systems, and cutting-edge innovations that have transformed our world. Learn about the role of electricity in sustainable energy solutions and its importance in shaping a greener future.

Prepare to be enthralled as you explore these extraordinary museums, unlocking the secrets and stories that have shaped Mulhouse's captivating heritage.

4.6: Parc de la Citadelle

ALSACE TRAVELS

Welcome to Parc de la Citadelle, a magnificent urban park nestled in the heart of the charming city of La Rochelle, France. With its picturesque landscapes, rich historical heritage, and an array of recreational activities, this park is a true haven for nature lovers and history enthusiasts alike. Spanning over 20 hectares, Parc de la Citadelle offers an idyllic escape from the bustling city streets, inviting visitors to relax, explore, and immerse themselves in the enchanting ambiance. In this part, we will delve into the park's captivating features, from its lush greenery and diverse flora to its iconic historical landmarks and cultural attractions. Join us on an unforgettable journey through Parc de la Citadelle!

A Glimpse of History

The roots of Parc de la Citadelle trace back to the 17th century when the citadel, or fortress, was built to protect the city from invasions. Today, the park serves as a testament to La Rochelle's rich historical past. As you wander through its tranquil pathways, you'll come across remnants of the fortress, such as the imposing Porte Royale, a magnificent gateway adorned with intricate architectural details. This gate serves as the park's main entrance and marks the beginning of a captivating journey into the park's treasures.

A Tapestry of Nature

Parc de la Citadelle is a true paradise for nature enthusiasts, offering a captivating blend of meticulously manicured gardens and sprawling green spaces. The park's centerpiece is the Jardin des Plantes, a botanical garden that showcases a diverse collection of plants, flowers, and trees. Take a stroll along its winding paths, breathing in the fragrant scents and marveling at the vibrant colors that surround you.

Adjacent to the Jardin des Plantes, you'll find the serene Lac des Cygnes, a charming lake adorned with graceful swans gliding on its shimmering surface. The lake provides a peaceful atmosphere, perfect for picnics or simply unwinding amidst nature's beauty. Don't forget to bring some breadcrumbs to feed the friendly ducks and swans!

For a more adventurous experience, head towards the Parcours Sportif, an outdoor fitness area equipped with exercise stations that cater to all fitness levels. Whether you're looking to jog, stretch, or engage in strength training, this section of the park offers an opportunity to stay active amidst breathtaking surroundings.

A Historical Journey

As you delve deeper into Parc de la Citadelle, the park's historical significance unfolds before your eyes. The Forteresse des Dames stands proudly, harking back to the medieval period. This fascinating structure served as a residence for noblewomen and offers a glimpse into the region's feudal past. Explore its well-preserved chambers and courtyards, imagining the tales of the past that echo within its walls.

Another architectural gem within the park is the Lantern Tower, or Tour de la Lanterne. This impressive tower, dating back to the 13th century, once served as a lighthouse guiding ships into the harbor. Climb its narrow spiral staircase to reach the top and be rewarded with breathtaking panoramic views of La Rochelle and its surroundings.

For a truly immersive experience, visit the Musée Maritime de La Rochelle, housed within the park's boundaries. This maritime museum provides insight into La Rochelle's maritime heritage, displaying a vast collection of artifacts, models, and interactive exhibits that tell the captivating stories of the city's seafaring past.

Cultural Delights

Parc de la Citadelle not only offers natural beauty and historical marvels but also hosts a range of cultural activities that will enrich your visit. The open-air amphitheater, Théâtre de Verdure, is a perfect venue for concerts, theatrical performances, and other cultural events that take place throughout the year. Check the park's schedule to see if there are any shows during your visit, as witnessing a performance amidst the park's enchanting surroundings is truly unforgettable.

For art enthusiasts, the park is home to several contemporary sculptures and installations that seamlessly blend with the natural landscape. Take a moment to appreciate the intricate craftsmanship and thought-provoking concepts behind these works of art, which add a unique dimension to the park's ambiance.

Family-Friendly Activities

Parc de la Citadelle caters to visitors of all ages, making it an ideal destination for families. The park features a dedicated children's playground, complete with slides, swings, and climbing frames, ensuring that the little ones can have a memorable time in a safe and enjoyable environment.

To engage children in an educational experience, visit the Aquarium La Rochelle, conveniently located near the park. This fascinating aquarium showcases a wide variety of marine life, allowing young explorers to learn about the wonders of the underwater world. From colorful fish to mesmerizing jellyfish, this immersive journey will spark curiosity and deepen their appreciation for marine ecosystems.

From its lush gardens and serene lakes to its awe-inspiring historical landmarks and vibrant cultural events, Parc de la Citadelle beckons travelers to immerse themselves in its allure. So, pack your bags, venture into this enchanting oasis, and embark on an unforgettable journey through the wonders of Parc de la Citadelle in La Rochelle, France.

The Vosges Mountains

Nestled in the northeastern part of France, the Vosges Mountains are a breathtaking range known for their natural beauty and rich biodiversity. Stretching over 430 kilometers from the Rhine Valley in the east to the Belfort Gap in the west, this mountain range offers an idyllic escape for travelers looking for outdoor experiences and a chance to get back in touch with nature.

5.1: Overview

The Vosges Mountains boast an average elevation of around 1,000 meters, with its highest peak, the Grand Ballon, standing tall at 1,424 meters. The region's diverse landscape is characterized by lush green valleys, dense forests, cascading waterfalls, and picturesque lakes. These mountains have been recognized as a regional natural park, emphasizing the significance of preserving their pristine beauty and unique ecosystems.

The Vosges Mountains have a rich cultural heritage, shaped by the influences of both French and German traditions. The region's distinctive architecture, cuisine, and folklore reflect this blend of cultures, offering travelers a captivating glimpse into the past. Exploring the charming villages and towns nestled amidst the mountains is a delightful way to immerse oneself in the local culture.

5.2: Hiking & Nature Trails

For avid hikers and nature enthusiasts, the Vosges Mountains offer an extensive network of trails that cater to all skill levels. Whether you're a seasoned mountaineer or a casual nature lover, there is a trail suited to your preferences and abilities. Lace up your boots, pack your backpack, and get ready to embark on an unforgettable journey through the Vosges wilderness.

Grandes Traversées des Vosges

One of the most renowned hiking routes in the Vosges Mountains is the Grandes

Traversées des Vosges (GTV). This long-distance trail spans over 400 kilometers, taking trekkers on an epic adventure through the heart of the mountain range. Divided into three main sections, the GTV offers a variety of landscapes and breathtaking vistas.

The Northern Vosges section of the GTV takes hikers through dense forests, stunning rock formations, and ancient ruins. Along the way, you'll encounter charming villages and towns, providing opportunities to rest, refuel, and learn about the local history and culture. The central section, known as the Central Vosges, showcases the region's picturesque lakes, including the serene Lac Blanc and Lac Noir. As you hike through this section, you'll be treated to panoramic views of the surrounding peaks and valleys. The Southern Vosges section, with its rolling hills and vast meadows, offers a tranquil and peaceful atmosphere, perfect for those seeking solitude in nature.

The GTV is well-marked and maintained, ensuring a safe and enjoyable experience for hikers. Along the route, you'll find accommodations ranging from mountain huts to cozy guesthouses, providing comfortable resting places after a day of exploration. It's advisable to plan your hike and check the weather conditions, as the Vosges Mountains can experience sudden climate changes.

The Route des Crêtes

For travelers seeking a shorter but equally rewarding hiking experience, the Route des Crêtes is an excellent choice. This iconic trail follows the ridgeline of the Vosges Mountains, offering unparalleled panoramic views of the surrounding landscape. Stretching approximately 80 kilometers from Cernay to Sainte-Marie-aux-Mines, the Route des Crêtes is easily accessible and can be completed in several days.

As you hike along the Route des Crêtes, you'll be captivated by the beauty of the Vosges Mountains. Marvel at the rugged cliffs, deep gorges, and sweeping vistas that unfold before you. Highlights along the trail include the Hohneck, the third-highest peak in the Vosges, and the stunning Lac de Blanchemer, a tranquil lake nestled amidst the mountains.

The Route des Crêtes is well-equipped with signposts and information boards, providing insights into the region's geology, flora, and fauna. It's important to come prepared with proper hiking gear, including sturdy footwear, sufficient water, and appropriate clothing for varying weather conditions.

Nature Trails & Interpretive Centers

Beyond the long-distance trails, the Vosges Mountains offer numerous nature trails and interpretive centers, providing opportunities for visitors to delve deeper into the region's natural wonders. These shorter trails are perfect for families, beginners, or those looking for a stroll amidst breathtaking scenery.

The Sentier des Roches (Rock Trail) is a popular choice among visitors, offering a unique opportunity to explore the fascinating rock formations that shape the Vosges landscape. The trail winds its way through the Petit Ballon massif, showcasing impressive sandstone cliffs, natural arches, and hidden caves. Along the way, interpretive panels provide valuable information about the geological history and ecological importance of the area.

If you're interested in the region's flora and fauna, the Sentier des Chaumes (Ridge Trail) is a must-visit. This trail meanders through the Ballons des Vosges Nature Reserve, a protected area renowned for its rich biodiversity. Keep your eyes peeled for rare orchids, colorful butterflies, and elusive bird species as you explore this enchanting trail.

To gain a deeper understanding of the Vosges Mountains' natural and cultural heritage, be sure to visit the interpretive centers scattered throughout the region. These centers offer interactive exhibits, educational displays, and guided tours, providing valuable insights into the area's history, geology, and ecology. The Parc Naturel Régional des Ballons des Vosges Visitor Center and the Maison de la Nature du Ried et de l'Alsace Centrale are particularly worth visiting for a comprehensive understanding of the region.

The Vosges Mountains are a true haven for hikers and nature enthusiasts, offering a diverse range of trails and breathtaking landscapes to explore. Whether you embark on the epic adventure of the Grandes Traversées des Vosges or opt for shorter nature trails, you're guaranteed to be captivated by the region's beauty. So, lace up your boots, breathe in the fresh mountain air, and immerse yourself in the splendor of the Vosges Mountains. Your unforgettable journey awaits!

5.3: Ski Resorts in Alsace

Alsace may not have towering alpine peaks, but it compensates with its charming ski resorts that cater to all skill levels. These resorts offer well-groomed slopes, excellent facilities, and a warm atmosphere that will make your winter escapades truly memorable. Here are a few noteworthy ski resorts in the region:

Lac Blanc Ski Resort

Nestled in the heart of the Vosges Mountains, Lac Blanc Ski Resort is a paradise for winter sports enthusiasts. It boasts 14 slopes covering various difficulty levels, providing ample opportunities for both beginners and experienced skiers. The resort's state-of-the-art lifts ensure efficient transportation, and its dedicated snowmaking system guarantees excellent snow conditions throughout the season. Lac Blanc also offers ski lessons for all ages and has a snow park for snowboarders and freestyle skiers. The breathtaking views of the surrounding mountains and the pristine Lac Blanc make this resort a true gem.

Lac des Truites Ski Resort

Situated near the picturesque town of Gerardmer, Lac des Truites Ski Resort is another fantastic destination for winter sports lovers. With 40 kilometers of ski slopes spread across diverse terrain, this resort has something for everyone. From gentle slopes for beginners to challenging runs for experts, skiers of all levels can enjoy a fulfilling experience here. Lac des Truites is known for its excellent snow conditions, thanks to its modern snow making facilities. The resort also offers cross-country skiing trails, snowshoeing routes, and a wide range of après-ski activities, ensuring an all-around winter adventure.

5.4: Lac Blanc & Lac des Truites

Alsace's natural beauty shines during the winter months, and two exceptional locations that capture this magic are Lac Blanc and Lac des Truites. These stunning lakes, surrounded by pristine forests and snow-covered peaks, offer breathtaking views and a serene atmosphere. Let's delve deeper into these locations:

Lac Blanc

Nestled in the Vosges Mountains, Lac Blanc is a glacial lake that exudes tranquility and natural splendor. During winter, the lake transforms into a mesmerizing frozen landscape, providing a unique opportunity for exploration. Cross-country skiers can venture around the lake, immersing themselves in the awe-inspiring winter scenery. For those seeking a more relaxed experience, walking or snowshoeing along the lake's shores offers a chance to appreciate the serenity of the surroundings. Lac Blanc is a true haven for nature enthusiasts and photographers alike, who can capture the beauty of the icy landscape.

Lac des Truites

Located near Gerardmer, Lac des Truites is another breathtaking winter destination in Alsace. The lake's calm surface reflects the snow-covered trees, creating a dreamlike ambiance. Cross-country skiing around the lake is a popular activity, allowing visitors to enjoy the solitude and beauty of the surroundings. Lac des Truites is also an excellent spot for ice fishing enthusiasts, who can indulge in this traditional winter pastime. The nearby town of Gerardmer offers cozy accommodations and a wide range of restaurants serving delicious local cuisine, making it an ideal base for exploring the area.

5.5: Grand Ballon d'Alsace

Rising majestically to a height of 1,424 meters, the Grand Ballon d'Alsace is the highest peak in the Vosges Mountains. It offers breathtaking panoramic views of the surrounding landscapes, making it a must-visit destination for nature lovers and adventure seekers. During the winter months, the Grand Ballon d'Alsace transforms into a winter wonderland, captivating visitors with its snow-clad slopes and stunning vistas.

Alpine Skiing

The Grand Ballon d'Alsace boasts several alpine skiing opportunities for all levels of expertise. From gentle slopes for beginners to challenging descents for experienced skiers, the resort offers a diverse range of options. The well-maintained slopes, coupled with the modern lift system, ensure a seamless skiing experience. Adrenaline junkies can also try their hand at freeriding, exploring the untouched powder snow off-piste.

Snowshoeing & Winter Hiking

For those who prefer a more leisurely pace, snowshoeing and winter hiking trails abound around the Grand Ballon d'Alsace. The snow-covered forests and meadows create a pristine setting for exploration. Guided tours are available for beginners, offering a chance to learn about the region's flora, fauna, and history while immersing oneself in the tranquility of the surroundings.

Paragliding & Hang Gliding

The Grand Ballon d'Alsace is a renowned destination for paragliding and hang gliding enthusiasts. The combination of favorable wind conditions and breathtaking views makes it an exhilarating experience. Admire the snow-capped peaks and valleys as you soar through the sky, enjoying an unmatched perspective of Alsace's winter beauty.

Nordic Skiing & Cross-Country Trails

The region surrounding the Grand Ballon d'Alsace is a paradise for cross-country skiing enthusiasts. Numerous well-maintained trails cater to all skill levels, offering an opportunity to explore the peaceful winter landscape at your own pace. Enjoy the rhythmic glide of skis on snow as you traverse through enchanting forests and valleys.

ALSACE TRAVELS

Alsace's winter wonderland beckons with its captivating ski resorts, serene lakes, and the majestic Grand Ballon d'Alsace. Whether you're seeking thrilling downhill slopes, peaceful cross-country trails, or breathtaking winter scenery, this region has it all. Discover the magic of Lac Blanc and Lac des Truites, where frozen landscapes and pristine forests create a picturesque backdrop. And don't miss the grandeur of the Grand Ballon d'Alsace, offering a diverse range of winter activities for all adventure enthusiasts. Plan your winter escape to Alsace, where unforgettable experiences await amidst the snow-clad beauty of this enchanting region.

ALSACE TRAVELS

ALSACE TRAVELS

Alsace Cuisine & Gastronomy

Renowned for its rich culinary heritage, Alsatian cuisine combines influences from French and German traditions, resulting in a unique and delectable gastronomic experience. In this guide, we will delve into the traditional dishes that define Alsatian cuisine and explore the region's world-famous wines and wineries. Prepare your taste buds for an unforgettable journey through the flavors of Alsace.

6.1: Traditional Alsatian Dishes

Choucroute Garnie

A quintessential Alsatian dish, Choucroute Garnie is a hearty combination of sauerkraut, potatoes, and a variety of meats such as sausages, pork, and smoked pork chops. This delicious dish reflects the region's Germanic influence and is often accompanied by mustard and boiled potatoes.

Flammekueche (Tarte Flambée)

A beloved Alsatian specialty, Flammekueche is a thin, crispy pizza-like tart topped with crème fraîche, onions, and bacon. The combination of the creamy base, caramelized onions, and smoky bacon creates a delightful balance of flavors.

Baeckeoffe

Baeckeoffe is a slow-cooked casserole that showcases the region's culinary heritage. It consists of layers of marinated lamb, beef, and pork, along with potatoes, leeks, onions, carrots, and aromatic herbs. Traditionally, the dish is cooked in a ceramic dish sealed with dough, allowing the flavors to meld together beautifully.

Fleischnacka

Fleischnacka are rolled pasta squares filled with a mixture of ground beef, onions, parsley, and spices. These savory delights are baked and then served with a creamy mushroom or tomato sauce. Fleischnacka is a favorite among locals and visitors alike.

Kougelhopf

No visit to Alsace is complete without indulging in Kougelhopf, a traditional Alsatian cake. This sweet, yeast-based brioche is often baked with raisins and almonds, creating a delightful texture and aroma. Kougelhopf is a popular treat for breakfast or as a dessert, and it pairs perfectly with a cup of coffee or a glass of Gewürztraminer wine.

Munster Cheese

Alsatian cuisine boasts an impressive array of cheeses, and Munster is one of the most famous varieties. This washed-rind cheese has a distinctively pungent aroma and a rich, creamy texture. It is often enjoyed on its own, with bread, or incorporated into various Alsatian dishes.

6.2: Wine & Wineries

The Alsace Wine Route

Embark on a scenic journey along the Alsace Wine Route, which stretches over 170 kilometers (105 miles) through picturesque vineyards, charming villages, and historical sites. This route is an excellent way to explore the region's wineries, sample exquisite wines, and learn about the winemaking process.

Grape Varieties

Alsace is renowned for its exceptional white wines, particularly those made from the region's four noble grape varieties: Riesling, Gewürztraminer, Pinot Gris, and Muscat. Each grape variety offers a unique flavor profile, from the crispness of Riesling to the aromatic and spicy notes of Gewürztraminer.

Wine Tastings

During your visit to Alsace, make sure to indulge in wine tastings at the numerous wineries and cellars dotted along the wine route. From small, family-run operations to large renowned estates, you will have the opportunity to sample a wide range of exquisite wines and discover your personal favorites.

Wine Festivals

Alsace is known for its vibrant wine festivals, which celebrate the region's viticultural heritage. The most famous festival is the Alsace Wine Fair in Colmar, held annually in July. This lively event showcases the finest wines of the region, accompanied by local cuisine, music, and traditional dances.

Crémant d'Alsace

Besides still wines, Alsace is also renowned for its sparkling wine, known as Crémant d'Alsace. Made using the traditional method, Crémant d'Alsace offers an excellent alternative to Champagne. Its fine bubbles, crispness, and delicate flavors make it a perfect aperitif or companion to festive celebrations.

Wineries to Visit

Several prestigious wineries in Alsace are worth exploring. Domaine Zind-Humbrecht in Turckheim is renowned for its biodynamic practices and exceptional wines, particularly Riesling and Gewürztraminer. Another notable winery is Domaine Marcel Deiss in Bergheim, which produces unique and expressive wines using a blend of grape varieties and terroirs.

As you immerse yourself in the culinary wonders of Alsace, be prepared to savor the region's traditional dishes that have stood the test of time. Indulge in the heartiness of Choucroute Garnie, the crispy perfection of Flammekueche, and the comforting flavors of Baeckeoffe. Pair these dishes with the exquisite wines of Alsace, from the floral and fruity Gewürztraminer to the elegant and versatile Riesling. And as you venture along the Alsace Wine Route, discover the charm of the region's wineries, where passion and tradition meet to produce wines that truly capture the essence of this remarkable region. Bon appétit and santé!

6.3: Beer & Breweries in Alsace

From traditional breweries to artisanal cheese producers, prepare to savor the distinct flavors and aromas that make Alsace a paradise for food and drink enthusiasts.

The Beer Tradition of Alsace

Beer has a long-standing tradition in Alsace, dating back centuries. Influenced by both German and French brewing techniques, Alsace has developed its own unique beer culture. The region is renowned for producing a variety of beer styles, including lagers, wheat beers, and hop-forward ales. The beers of Alsace are characterized by their exceptional quality, rich flavors, and adherence to traditional brewing methods.

Traditional Breweries in Alsace

Alsace is home to several traditional breweries that have been crafting beer for generations. These breweries pride themselves on using high-quality ingredients sourced from the region, resulting in beers that truly reflect the terroir of Alsace. Some notable breweries include Brasserie Kronenbourg, which has been operating since 1664 and is famous for its Kronenbourg 1664 lager. Another iconic brewery is Brasserie Sainte Cru, known for its range of artisanal beers made with local hops and barley.

Craft Beer Revolution in Alsace

In recent years, Alsace has witnessed a craft beer revolution, with a surge in microbreweries and brewpubs that offer innovative and experimental brews. These establishments focus on small-scale production, allowing them to push the boundaries of traditional beer styles. Craft breweries like Brasserie Perle and Brasserie

Uberach have gained recognition for their dedication to quality and creativity, producing a wide array of flavorful and unique beers that cater to diverse palates.

Beer Tasting Experiences in Alsace

Immerse yourself in the beer culture of Alsace by embarking on beer-tasting experiences across the region. Many breweries offer guided tours, allowing visitors to learn about the brewing process, explore historic cellars, and, of course, sample a variety of beers. Take the opportunity to interact with passionate brewers, who are eager to share their knowledge and stories behind each brew. Whether you're a seasoned beer enthusiast or a curious novice, these tastings provide a delightful insight into the rich brewing heritage of Alsace.

Beer & Food Pairing in Alsace

ALSACE TRAVELS

Beer and food pairing is an integral part of the Alsace culinary experience. The region's diverse beer styles offer a myriad of possibilities when it comes to enhancing the flavors of local dishes. Pair a light and crisp lager with tarte flambée, a traditional Alsatian flatbread topped with cream, onions, and bacon. For heartier fare like choucroute garnie (sauerkraut with various types of meat), opt for a malty amber ale or a rich stout. The unique interplay between Alsace's beer and cuisine is a testament to the region's commitment to gastronomic excellence.

6.4: Alsatian Cheeses

The Art of Cheese-making in Alsace

Cheese-making in Alsace is a true art form, deeply rooted in tradition and craftsmanship. The region's fertile lands, coupled with its rich dairy farming heritage, provide an ideal environment for producing exceptional cheeses. From creamy soft cheeses to pungent blues, Alsace offers a diverse range of cheese varieties that captivate the senses.

Munster: The King of Alsatian Cheeses

Munster cheese, one of the most iconic Alsatian cheeses, takes center stage in the region's cheese-making scene. This washed-rind cheese is characterized by its pungent aroma and creamy texture. Produced primarily from cow's milk, Munster develops its distinct flavors during the aging process, which can last from a few weeks to several months. Delve into the world of Munster cheese and discover the nuances of its taste profiles, from mild and buttery to intensely savory.

Alsatian Soft Cheeses

In addition to Munster, Alsace produces a delightful array of soft cheeses. One such example is the renowned Tomme d'Alsace, a semi-soft cheese with a bloomy rind and a creamy interior. Its delicate flavors pair wonderfully with crusty bread and fresh fruits. Other soft cheeses like Sainte-Marie-aux-Mines and Marcaire offer unique taste experiences, showcasing the diversity and creativity of Alsatian cheese-making.

Blue Cheese from Alsace

Blue cheese lovers are in for a treat when exploring Alsace's cheese offerings. The region produces exceptional blue cheeses, such as Bleu d'Alsace and Bleu des Vosges. These cheeses feature a beautiful marbled appearance and a rich, complex flavor profile. Their creamy texture and distinctive tangy notes make them a perfect choice for cheese boards or as an ingredient in savory dishes.

As you explore the beer and cheese culture of Alsace, you will embark on a remarkable gastronomic journey. From traditional breweries steeped in history to innovative craft beer pioneers, Alsace offers an impressive range of beers to satisfy every palate. Complementing the beer scene, Alsatian cheeses, led by the iconic Munster, showcase the region's cheese-making expertise. Immerse yourself in the rich flavors, aromas, and traditions of Alsace, and let the beer and cheese captivate your senses, leaving an indelible mark on your culinary adventures. Cheers, and bon appétit!

6.5: Food Festivals & Markets

Alsace Wine & Gastronomy Fair

Indulge in a celebration of Alsace's finest wines and culinary delights at the Alsace

Wine and Gastronomy Fair. Held annually in Colmar, this festival brings together local winemakers, producers, and chefs. Immerse yourself in the vibrant atmosphere as you sample a wide array of wines, cheeses, sausages, and pastries. Engage in wine tastings, attend cooking demonstrations by renowned chefs, and explore the stalls offering regional specialties. This festival is a true feast for the senses, allowing you to discover the essence of Alsace's gastronomy.

Munster Cheese Festival

Munster cheese, a pungent and creamy delicacy, takes center stage at the Munster Cheese Festival in the picturesque village of Munster. This annual event celebrates the region's famous cheese, offering visitors a chance to taste and learn about its production. Explore the cheese market, meet local farmers and cheesemakers, and witness the fascinating cheese-making process. From sampling a variety of Munster cheese preparations to savoring cheese-inspired dishes, this festival is a must-visit for cheese lovers seeking an authentic Alsace experience.

Strasbourg Christmas Market

Step into a magical winter wonderland at the Strasbourg Christmas Market, one of the oldest and most renowned Christmas markets in Europe. Amidst the festive ambiance, immerse yourself in the aromas of gingerbread, mulled wine, and roasted chestnuts. Stroll through the charming stalls adorned with Christmas decorations and discover a wide range of traditional Alsace delicacies. From foie gras and spiced bread to bredele (Alsatian Christmas cookies), this market offers a delightful journey through Alsace's culinary traditions during the holiday season.

Asparagus Festival

In the small village of Hoerdt, Alsace pays homage to its beloved white asparagus with the annual Asparagus Festival. Explore the bustling market stalls brimming with freshly harvested asparagus, and savor this delicate vegetable in a myriad of mouthwatering preparations. From creamy soups and quiches to asparagus-topped tarts and gratins, the festival showcases the versatility and delectable flavors of this local specialty. Immerse yourself in the lively ambiance, participate in cooking competitions, and revel in the unique charm of the Asparagus Festival.

Obernai Market

Located in the charming town of Obernai, this market offers a delightful selection of local produce, artisanal products, and regional specialties. Stroll through the market stalls filled with colorful fruits, vegetables, cheeses, cured meats, and freshly baked goods. Immerse yourself in the vibrant atmosphere as you interact with local vendors and sample the flavors of Alsace.

Mulhouse Market

The Mulhouse Market, held in the heart of the city, is a bustling hub of culinary delights. This vibrant market showcases a diverse range of fresh produce, including fruits, vegetables, herbs, and spices. Browse through the stalls to discover an assortment of homemade preserves, aromatic oils, and artisanal products. The market also features international flavors, reflecting Mulhouse's multiculturalism.

Ribeauvillé Market

Nestled in the picturesque town of Ribeauvillé, this market offers a charming setting to explore local gastronomy. Wander through the narrow streets and browse the stalls offering regional specialties such as sausages, sauerkraut, honey, and gingerbread. Admire the beautifully presented fruits and vegetables, and don't miss the opportunity to sample some of Alsace's famous wines from nearby vineyards.

Saint-Louis Market

Located near the borders of France, Germany, and Switzerland, the Saint-Louis Market is a melting pot of flavors and cultures. This vibrant market showcases a diverse range of international products, reflecting the region's cross-cultural influences. Explore the stalls offering exotic spices, ethnic foods, and a variety of international ingredients. From Middle Eastern delicacies to Asian spices, this market is a paradise for adventurous food lovers.

Wissembourg Market

Situated in the charming town of Wissembourg, this traditional market offers a glimpse into Alsace's agricultural heritage. Browse through the stalls to discover an array of locally grown fruits, vegetables, herbs, and flowers. Sample regional cheeses, cured meats, and freshly baked loaves of bread. The market's cozy and friendly atmosphere makes it a perfect place to connect with local producers and experience the authentic flavors of Alsace.

6.6: Culinary Workshops

Le Cordon Bleu, Strasbourg

For those seeking a world-class culinary education, Le Cordon Bleu in Strasbourg is an unrivaled destination. With its rich culinary heritage, Alsace serves as an ideal backdrop for honing your culinary skills. Join expert chefs in hands-on workshops and master the art of Alsatian cuisine. From learning the secrets of tarte flambée and choucroute garnie to perfecting delicate pastries like kougelhopf and pain d'épices, these workshops provide an immersive and educational experience for aspiring chefs and culinary enthusiasts.

Cooking Classes at Maison Kammerzell, Strasbourg

Embark on a gastronomic journey at Maison Kammerzell, a historic restaurant in Strasbourg. Offering a range of cooking classes, this renowned establishment allows you to delve into the intricacies of Alsatian cuisine. Under the guidance of skilled chefs, discover the techniques behind iconic dishes such as baeckeoffe (meat and vegetable casserole) and coq au Riesling (chicken in Riesling wine). The classes provide a unique opportunity to learn from culinary experts and gain a deeper understanding of Alsace's culinary heritage.

Alsace Wine Route: Vineyard Experiences

Explore the scenic Alsace Wine Route and uncover the secrets of winemaking through immersive vineyard experiences. Join local winemakers in hands-on activities such as grape harvesting, wine blending, and cellar tours. Gain insights into the region's grape varieties, terroir, and winemaking techniques. As you sample a variety of wines, from crisp Rieslings to luscious Gewürztraminers, deepen your appreciation for Alsace's rich viticultural traditions. These experiences offer a perfect blend of wine education and cultural immersion.

Traditional Bread Baking Workshops

Delve into the art of breadmaking with traditional bread-baking workshops held in various towns and villages across Alsace. Learn from skilled bakers as they guide you through the process of creating iconic

Alsatian bread, such as pain d'épices (spice bread) and pretzels. Discover the importance of local ingredients and traditional techniques in achieving the perfect crust and texture. These workshops provide a unique opportunity to connect with Alsace's culinary heritage and take home the skills to recreate authentic Alsatian bread.

Alsace's food festivals, markets, and culinary workshops offer an exceptional opportunity to explore the region's rich gastronomic traditions. Whether you're a wine connoisseur, a cheese lover, or an aspiring chef, Alsace's vibrant culinary scene will captivate your senses. Immerse yourself in the lively atmosphere of food festivals, sample local delicacies at bustling markets, and refine your culinary skills through immersive workshops. Embrace the flavors of Alsace, and let this remarkable region awaken your taste buds to a world of gastronomic delights.

ALSACE TRAVELS

Off the Beaten Path

While popular attractions like Strasbourg and Colmar often steal the limelight, numerous offbeat destinations are waiting to be explored. In this guide, we will take you on a journey through some of the lesser-known treasures of Alsace, each with its own unique story to tell. From the majestic Haut-Koenigsbourg Castle to the serene Mont Sainte-Odile and the poignant Struthof Concentration Camp, prepare to be captivated by the richness of Alsace's history, culture, and natural beauty.

7.1: Offbeat Destinations in Alsace

Eguisheim

Tucked away in the vineyard-draped hills, Eguisheim is a postcard-perfect medieval village. Its narrow, winding streets, half-timbered houses, and colorful flower displays create a fairytale ambiance. Take a stroll and soak in the medieval charm while discovering local artisanal shops and family-owned wineries.

Riquewihr

Step into the past as you explore the enchanting village of Riquewihr. Enclosed by well-preserved medieval fortifications, this village transports you to a bygone era. Admire the ornate facades of the half-timbered houses, visit the historical museum, and indulge in a tasting of the region's famous Gewürztraminer wine.

Obernai

Nestled in the foothills of the Vosges Mountains, Obernai is a hidden gem that combines history and natural beauty. Explore the cobblestone streets that are lined with vibrant, flower-adorned buildings. Explore the medieval ramparts, visit the St. Odile Church, and savor the local cuisine at one of the charming cafés.

Turckheim

Known as the "Village with the Witch," Turckheim is a small town with a bewitching charm. Take a guided tour to uncover its secrets and legends, including the story of the witch who saved the town from invaders. Enjoy a glass of local wine at one of the traditional wineries and be enchanted by the town's well-preserved medieval gateways.

7.2: Haut-Koenigsbourg Castle

Perched on a hilltop in the Vosges Mountains, Haut-Koenigsbourg Castle stands as a testament to Alsace's rich history. This imposing medieval fortress offers a glimpse into the region's turbulent past. Dating back to the 12th century, the castle has undergone extensive restoration and is now open to the public.

Step through the castle gates and enter a world of knights, royalty, and strategic warfare. Explore the various rooms, from the grand hall to the armory, and marvel at the architectural details. Don't miss the panoramic views of the Alsace plains and the Black Forest from the castle's towers.

Immerse yourself in the castle's history through engaging exhibits that showcase medieval life, weaponry, and siege techniques. Knowledgeable guides bring the past to life, regaling visitors with stories of power struggles and heroic deeds.

For an even deeper experience, participate in one of the castle's themed events, such as medieval festivals or knight tournaments.

ALSACE TRAVELS

Witness knights in armor, falconry displays, and traditional music transporting you back to the castle's heyday.

7.3: Mont Sainte-Odile

High above the Alsace plain, Mont Sainte-Odile offers a peaceful retreat amidst lush forests and breathtaking vistas. This sacred mountain has been a place of pilgrimage for centuries, attracting visitors seeking tranquility and spiritual solace.

At the heart of Mont Sainte-Odile sits the majestic Odile Abbey, an architectural gem dating back to the 8th century. Wander through the cloistered courtyard and explore the abbey's interior, adorned with intricate frescoes and sculptures. The panoramic terrace provides awe-inspiring views of the Alsace countryside.

Follow the paths that wind through the forest, leading to the holy spring and the Chapelle des Larmes (Chapel of Tears). Legend has it that these tears shed by Saint Odile, the abbey's patron saint, possess healing powers. Take a moment of reflection at the chapel and soak in the serene atmosphere.

For a deeper understanding of the abbey's history and significance, visit the nearby Mont Sainte-Odile Museum. Discover artifacts, manuscripts, and archaeological findings that shed light on the mountain's past.

7.4: Struthof Concentration Camp

While not an easy visit, the Struthof Concentration Camp is a poignant reminder of the darkest chapters in human history. Located in the Vosges Mountains, this former Nazi concentration camp is now a memorial and museum dedicated to honoring the victims and educating future generations.

Explore the somber grounds and visit the various buildings, such as the crematorium, gas chamber, and barracks. The museum exhibits provide a comprehensive account of the camp's history, recounting the suffering endured by prisoners and the atrocities committed.

Engage with the exhibits that detail the daily life of prisoners, their stories of resistance, and the horrors they faced. Gain a deeper understanding of the Holocaust and reflect on the importance of remembrance and tolerance.

Attend one of the educational programs or guided tours offered at the site to delve further into the camp's history. Expert guides provide context, personal stories, and insights, ensuring a meaningful and respectful visit.

Take a moment to pay your respects at the monument and memorial site, honoring the memory of those who perished at Struthof. The serene surroundings serve as a reminder of the importance of preserving human dignity and promoting peace.

We hope that these offbeat destinations have provided you with a deeper appreciation for the region's rich history, culture, and natural beauty. From the fairytale-like villages of Eguisheim and Riquewihr to the historical significance of Haut-Koenigsbourg Castle, Mont Sainte-Odile, and the Struthof Concentration Camp, each destination offers a unique experience.

While Alsace's more popular attractions may steal the spotlight, venturing off the beaten path allows you to discover hidden gems and delve into lesser-known aspects of this captivating region. Whether you seek medieval charm, spiritual tranquility, or a somber reminder of the past, Alsace has something to offer every traveler.

7.5: Rhine River

As one of Europe's most iconic waterways, the Rhine flows through six countries, captivating all who venture along its banks. This comprehensive guide aims to provide you with an immersive and insightful experience, covering the river's history, culture, and breathtaking natural landscapes. So, sit back, relax, and prepare to embark on an unforgettable journey along the majestic Rhine.

Historical Significance

Ancient Origins & Roman Influence

The Rhine River has played a pivotal role throughout history, serving as a natural boundary and trade route. Its significance can be traced back to ancient times when the Romans first recognized its strategic importance. They established settlements along its banks and constructed forts, leaving behind a rich cultural legacy.

Middle Ages & the Rhine Trade Route

During the Middle Ages, the Rhine became a bustling trade route, connecting major cities such as Cologne, Mainz, and Strasbourg. Merchants traded goods, including wine, textiles, and precious metals, contributing to the economic prosperity of the region. Magnificent castles and fortifications still stand as reminders of this prosperous era.

Romanticism & the Loreley

The Rhine's romantic allure is captured in folklore and literary works, particularly in the legendary tale of the Loreley. This mythical siren, said to have bewitched sailors with her enchanting song, has become an emblem of the river's captivating charm. The Romantic period further enhanced the Rhine's reputation as a source of inspiration for poets, painters, and musicians.

Cultural Heritage

UNESCO World Heritage Sites

The Rhine River is home to several UNESCO World Heritage Sites that showcase its cultural wealth. From the Cologne Cathedral's Gothic splendor to the breathtaking Rhine Gorge, with its vineyards and picturesque villages, these sites offer a glimpse into centuries of human ingenuity and creativity.

Vineyards & Wine Culture

The fertile valleys along the Rhine are renowned for their vineyards, which produce some of Europe's finest wines. Explore the wine-growing regions of the Moselle, Rheingau, and Alsace, and indulge in tastings of Riesling, Gewürztraminer, and Pinot Noir. Immerse yourself in the wine culture, attend wine festivals, and learn about the art of viticulture.

Rhine Festivals & Traditions

Throughout the year, the Rhine region comes alive with vibrant festivals and age-old traditions. Experience the colorful Carnival celebrations in Cologne, witness the traditional wine festivals in Rüdesheim, or immerse yourself in the folklore during the Rhine in Flames fireworks displays. These events provide a unique opportunity to embrace the local customs and immerse yourself in the region's rich cultural tapestry.

ALSACE TRAVELS

Natural Beauty

The Rhine Valley & its Landscapes

Embark on a scenic journey through the Rhine Valley, a breathtaking stretch between Mainz and Bonn. Marvel at the picturesque landscapes, where vine-clad hillsides, medieval castles, and charming villages create an idyllic setting. The Rhine Gorge, with its dramatic cliffs and the legendary Loreley rock, stands out as a highlight of this remarkable region.

The Upper Middle Rhine Valley

Recognized as a UNESCO World Heritage Site, the Upper Middle Rhine Valley is a true gem. Its terraced vineyards, rugged cliffs, and charming towns transport you to a bygone era. Take a river cruise, explore the quaint streets of Bacharach and Boppard, and enjoy panoramic views from the imposing Marksburg Castle.

ALSACE TRAVELS

Natural Parks & Outdoor Activities

For nature enthusiasts, the Rhine region offers an array of outdoor activities. Discover the tranquility of the Rhine-Taunus Nature Park, hike through the Siebengebirge's lush forests, or cycle along the scenic Rhine Cycle Path. Indulge in birdwatching, canoeing, or simply relax in one of the many riverside parks.

As your journey along the Rhine River comes to an end, we hope this guide has provided you with valuable insights into the historical, cultural, and natural wonders that await you. From ancient Roman settlements to fairy-tale castles and world-class vineyards, the Rhine River offers an unparalleled experience that will leave a lasting imprint on your heart. So, pack your bags, embark on this remarkable adventure, and let the Rhine weave its magic

ALSACE TRAVELS

as you explore its captivating landscapes and immerse yourself in its rich heritage.

ALSACE TRAVELS

Practical Information

As a traveler venturing into this enchanting region, it is helpful to familiarize yourself with the local language, communication practices, and useful phrases to enhance your experience.

8.1: Language, Communication & Useful Phrases

Alsace is a bilingual region, where both French and Alsatian, a German dialect, are widely spoken. French is the official language, but many locals are fluent in both languages, particularly in rural areas. While it is possible to get by with English in major tourist destinations, making an effort to learn a few basic phrases in French or Alsatian will undoubtedly enhance your interactions with locals and demonstrate your respect for their culture.

Basic Phrases

Here are some essential phrases to help you navigate Alsace:

- → Hello (General Greeting): French: Bonjour Alsatian: Griessech / Salü

- → Goodbye: French: Au revoir Alsatian: Wiederluege / Tschüss

- → Please: French: S'il vous plaît Alsatian: Gfallt mer / S'fleesch

- → Thank you: French: Merci Alsatian: Merci / Danke

- → Yes: French: Oui Alsatian: Joh / Ja

- → No: French: Non Alsatian: Nai / Nee

- → Excuse me: French: Excusez-moi Alsatian: Esch me / Verzeiht

- → I don't understand: French: Je ne comprends pas Alsatian: Ich versti-nitt / Ich verschtann nit

- → Do you speak English?: French: Parlez-vous anglais ? Alsatian: Schwätze Sie Englisch ? / Redde Sie Englisch ?

Greetings & Polite Expressions

When engaging with locals in Alsace, using appropriate greetings and polite expressions will go a long way in fostering positive interactions. Here are a few phrases to help you connect with the Alsatian people:

- → How are you?: French: Comment ça va ? Alsatian: Wie geht's ? / Wie geht's dir ?

- → I'm fine, thank you: French: Je vais bien, merci Alsatian: Mir gitt's guet, merci / Mir gitt's guet, danke

- → What is your name?: French: Comment vous appelez-vous ? Alsatian: Wie heisse Sie ? / Wie heisse Sie fer'n' Noame ?

- → My name is...: French: Je m'appelle... Alsatian: Ich heisse... / Ich haas...

- → Nice to meet you: French: Enchanté(e) Alsatian: Fröit mi / Fröit mi's / Fröit mi Sie kennen ze lerne

Ordering Food & Drinks

Alsace is renowned for its delectable cuisine and world-class wines. When dining out, these phrases will assist you in ordering food and drinks:

ALSACE TRAVELS

- → I would like...: French: Je voudrais... Alsatian: Ich hätt gärn... / Ich miät gärn...

- → What do you recommend?: French: Qu'est-ce que vous recommandez ? Alsatian: Was empfiehlt'sch ? / Was empfiehlt Sie ?

- → The bill, please: French: L'addition, s'il vous plaît Alsatian: Die Rechnung, bitte / S'groosss Rechnung, bitte

- → Cheers!: French: Santé ! Alsatian: Proscht ! / Proschteli !

- → A glass of wine, please: French: Un verre de vin, s'il vous plaît Alsatian: E glas Wìn, bitte / E glass Wìn, bitte

Directions & Transportation

Navigating through Alsace's enchanting towns and cities requires some knowledge of

ALSACE TRAVELS

directions and transportation. The following phrases will prove invaluable:

- Where is...?: French: Où se trouve... ? Alsatian: Wo isch... ? / Wo isch's... ?

- Train station: French: La gare Alsatian: S'Bahnhüsli / S'Bahnhüüsli

- Bus station: French: L'arrêt de bus Alsatian: S'Busswartestell / S'Busshaltställi

- Left: French: À gauche Alsatian: Linsk / Linsk ab

- Right: French: À droite Alsatian: Rinks / Rinks ab

- Straight ahead: French: Tout droit Alsatian: Uff d'Mitte zue / S'geradeus wyter

→ How much is the ticket?: French: Combien coûte le billet ? Alsatian: Wie viel koscht s'Billett ? / Wie viel koscht's Billett ?

Cultural Tips

Understanding the cultural nuances of Alsace will help you immerse yourself in the local way of life. Here are a few tips:

1. Embrace the Bilingualism: Appreciate the bilingual nature of the region and try using both French and Alsatian phrases when conversing with locals.

2. Be Polite: Politeness is highly valued in Alsace. Remember to greet people with a smile and use "please" and "thank you" when interacting with locals.

3. Enjoy the Gastronomy: Indulge in the region's culinary delights, such as

choucroute garnie (sauerkraut with sausages and other meats) and flammekueche (thin pizza-like tart). Pair them with local wines like Riesling or Gewürztraminer for an authentic experience.

4. Respect Local Customs: Respect local traditions and customs, such as observing quiet hours (known as "nuit calme") in residential areas and refraining from loud behavior.

5. Explore the Wine Route: Take the opportunity to explore the famous Alsace Wine Route, which winds through picturesque vineyards and charming villages. Enjoy wine tastings and learn about the region's winemaking heritage.

Alsace offers a fascinating blend of French and German cultures, and familiarizing yourself with the language and communication practices will undoubtedly enhance your travel experience. Remember to embrace bilingualism, be polite, and immerse yourself in the region's gastronomy and traditions. With these practical phrases and cultural tips, you can confidently navigate Alsace and connect with the locals on a deeper level, creating cherished memories of your time in this captivating region.

8.2: Currency & Banking

The Euro

Alsace, like the rest of France, uses the euro (€) as its official currency. It is advisable to familiarize yourself with the different euro banknotes and coins to avoid any confusion during transactions.

Currency Exchange

Currency exchange services are widely available in Alsace. You can exchange your currency at banks, post offices, and authorized currency exchange offices known as "bureaux de change." It's advisable to compare exchange rates and fees before choosing a provider. ATMs are also prevalent and offer competitive rates. The majority of businesses accept major payment cards.

Tipping

Tipping is not mandatory in France, but it is customary to leave a small tip for good service. A gratuity of 5-10% of the total bill is appreciated in restaurants, cafés, and taxis. Make sure to check if a service charge is already included in your bill, as it is common in some places.

Opening a Bank Account

If you're planning an extended stay in Alsace, opening a bank account can be beneficial. You will need to provide identification documents, proof of address, and proof of income or employment. Major French banks, such as BNP Paribas, Crédit Agricole, and Société Générale, have branches in Alsace. English-speaking staff can assist you in the process.

ATMs & Cash Withdrawals

Automated Teller Machines (ATMs) are widely available throughout Alsace, making it convenient to withdraw cash. Most ATMs accept major international cards, including Visa, Mastercard, and Maestro. Keep in mind that some ATMs may charge withdrawal fees, so check with your bank regarding any associated charges.

Online Banking & Mobile Apps

French banks provide online banking services, allowing you to manage your accounts, make transfers, and pay bills electronically. Many banks also offer mobile apps for added convenience. Ensure you have a secure internet connection when accessing online banking services.

Currency Exchange at Banks

While most banks in Alsace provide currency exchange services, it's advisable to check their rates and fees compared to specialized bureaux de change. Banks generally have limited hours for currency exchange, so plan accordingly.

Traveler's Checks

Traveler's checks are not widely accepted in Alsace. It is recommended to carry a combination of cash and cards for your financial needs. Inform your bank about your travel plans to ensure your cards are not blocked due to suspected fraudulent activity.

Emergencies & Lost Cards

In case of a lost or stolen card, promptly notify your bank to block the card and avoid unauthorized transactions. It is wise to carry a backup card or have access to emergency funds for unforeseen circumstances.

8.3: Transportation in Alsace

Public Transportation

Alsace has an efficient and well-connected public transportation system that includes buses, trams, and trains. The key cities of Strasbourg, Colmar, and Mulhouse have extensive networks, providing easy access to popular tourist destinations within the region.

Buses

The bus network in Alsace covers both urban and rural areas, connecting towns and villages. The buses are comfortable and equipped with modern facilities. Timetables and route information can be obtained from local tourist offices or transport authority websites. Tickets can be purchased from the driver or automated machines at bus stops.

Trams

Strasbourg boasts an excellent tram system that is convenient for getting around the city. The network covers major attractions, business districts, and residential areas. Tram tickets can be purchased from machines at tram stops or via mobile apps.

Trains

The train network in Alsace is operated by the French national railway company,

SNCF. It provides fast and efficient connections between major cities in Alsace and other regions of France. The TGV (high-speed train) is an excellent option for long-distance travel. Train tickets can be purchased online, at train stations, or via mobile apps.

Car Rental

If you prefer the flexibility of a car, rental services are available in Alsace. Major car rental companies have offices at airports, train stations, and city centers. Ensure you have a valid driver's license and check if an international driver's permit is required. Parking facilities are available in towns and cities, but it is advisable to familiarize yourself with parking regulations.

Cycling

Alsace is renowned for its picturesque countryside and vineyards, making it a perfect destination for cycling enthusiasts. You can rent bicycles in various towns and cities, and some accommodations provide bicycles for guests. Cycling routes are well-marked, and tourist offices can provide maps and guidance.

Taxis

Taxis are readily available in Alsace, particularly in urban areas and at transport hubs. Taxis operate on a metered system, and additional charges may apply for luggage or late-night journeys. It's recommended to use licensed taxis and ask for an estimated fare before starting the journey.

Alsace offers a diverse range of experiences, and understanding the local currency, banking services, and transportation options will enhance your visit to this captivating region. Remember to exchange your currency at reputable providers, consider opening a local bank account for extended stays, and utilize the convenient public transportation system.

8.4: Accommodation Options

Selecting the ideal lodging is essential for a special trip to this magical location when making travel plans. In this guide, we will explore the diverse range of accommodation options available in Alsace, ensuring you find the perfect place to stay that suits your preferences and budget.

Hotels

Alsace offers a wide array of hotels catering to various budgets and preferences. From luxurious five-star establishments to cozy boutique hotels, you'll find a plethora of options throughout the region. Strasbourg, the capital of Alsace, boasts numerous upscale hotels offering top-notch amenities and exceptional service. Colmar, another charming city in the region, is home to quaint hotels with a blend of traditional Alsatian architecture and modern comforts. Additionally, smaller towns and villages throughout Alsace offer charming family-run hotels, providing a more intimate and personalized experience.

Guesthouses & Bed & Breakfasts

For those seeking a more intimate and local experience, guesthouses and bed & breakfasts (B&Bs) are an excellent choice. Alsace is known for its warm hospitality, and staying in a guesthouse or B&B allows you to immerse yourself in the region's rich cultural heritage. These accommodations often provide cozy rooms with personalized touches and homemade breakfasts featuring regional specialties. The owners are usually friendly locals who can offer insider tips and recommendations for exploring Alsace's hidden gems.

Holiday Rentals & Apartments

Holiday rentals and apartments are ideal for travelers looking for more independence and flexibility. Alsace offers a variety of rental options, ranging from fully equipped apartments in the heart of cities like Strasbourg and Colmar to charming countryside cottages and gîtes (self-catering accommodations). This option allows you to experience Alsace at your own pace, with the convenience of having your own kitchen and living space. It is particularly suitable for families or groups of friends traveling together.

Wine Estates & Vineyard Stays

Alsace is renowned for its world-class wines, and staying at a wine estate or vineyard allows you to indulge in the region's viticultural heritage. Several wineries offer charming accommodations, providing a unique opportunity to experience the winemaking process firsthand. These accommodations often come with stunning views of the vineyards, wine tastings, and the chance to learn from passionate winemakers. It's an unforgettable way to delve into Alsace's wine culture while enjoying a peaceful and idyllic setting.

Castles & Châteaux

For a truly regal experience, consider staying in one of Alsace's magnificent castles or châteaux. The region boasts an impressive number of beautifully restored castles that have been converted into hotels. These accommodations offer a blend of history, elegance, and comfort, transporting you back in time while enjoying modern amenities. From opulent suites to grand dining halls, these castles and châteaux provide a unique and memorable stay for those seeking a touch of luxury and romance.

Camping & Outdoor Accommodations

Nature lovers and outdoor enthusiasts will find numerous camping options in Alsace. The region offers well-equipped campsites surrounded by lush greenery, with facilities ranging from basic to full-service. Camping in Alsace allows you to immerse yourself in the region's natural beauty, whether you prefer setting up a tent, parking your camper van, or staying in comfortable mobile homes. Many campsites also offer recreational activities, such as hiking and cycling trails, swimming pools, and playgrounds.

Wellness Retreats & Spas

Alsace is home to several wellness retreats and spas, perfect for those seeking relaxation and rejuvenation. These accommodations focus on providing a serene environment, wellness programs, and various spa treatments. You can unwind in thermal baths, indulge in massages and beauty treatments, or practice yoga and meditation. Whether you choose a countryside retreat or a spa in a bustling city, these accommodations offer a sanctuary for your mind, body, and soul.

Booking the Perfect Accommodation

With a variety of options available, it's important to consider your preferences, budget and desired location. Here, we will walk you through the steps of booking the perfect accommodation in Alsace, ensuring a stress-free experience.

Research & Planning

Start by researching the different areas of Alsace and identifying the cities, towns, or villages that align with your interests and itinerary. Consider factors such as proximity to attractions, transportation options, and the ambiance you desire. Once you have a shortlist of preferred locations, research the accommodation options available in those areas.

Set Your Budget

Determine your budget for accommodation and allocate a realistic amount for each night of your stay. Keep in mind that prices may vary depending on the season and the type of accommodation. Alsace offers options for various budgets, from luxury hotels to more budget-friendly guesthouses and holiday rentals.

Determine Your Accommodation Type

Consider the type of accommodation that suits your needs and preferences. Would you prefer a hotel for convenience and services, a guesthouse for a more personal experience, a holiday rental for independence, or a unique stay in a wine estate or castle? Knowing your preferred accommodation type will narrow down your search and simplify the booking process.

Check Online Booking Platforms

Utilize online booking platforms to explore a wide range of accommodation options in Alsace. Websites such as Booking.com, Expedia, and Airbnb provide comprehensive listings with detailed descriptions, reviews, and photos. Filter your search based on location, price range, amenities, and guest ratings to find suitable options.

Read Reviews & Ratings

Before making a final decision, read reviews and ratings from previous guests. Pay attention to comments about cleanliness, comfort, location, and the overall experience. Authentic reviews provide valuable insights and help you make an informed decision.

Contact the Accommodation

If you have specific questions or requirements, don't hesitate to contact the accommodation directly. Reach out via email or phone to inquire about availability, amenities, parking facilities, or any other concerns you may have. The staff will be happy to assist you and provide additional information.

Compare Prices & Policies

Once you have narrowed down your choices, compare prices and cancellation policies. Some accommodations offer flexible cancellation options, while others may require a deposit or have stricter cancellation policies. Take note of any additional fees, such as tourist taxes or parking charges, to avoid surprises during your stay.

Book & Confirm

When you have found the perfect accommodation that meets your requirements and fits your budget, proceed with the booking. Follow the instructions on the booking platform or contact the accommodation directly to confirm your reservation. Keep a copy of your confirmation details for reference.

Consider Additional Services & Amenities

Before your arrival, consider any additional services or amenities you may need. Do you require airport transfers, breakfast, or assistance with booking local tours? Contact the accommodation in advance to arrange these services and ensure a smooth and enjoyable stay.

Enjoy Your Stay

Congratulations, you've successfully booked your accommodation in Alsace! Upon arrival, check-in, in and acquaint yourself with the property and its surroundings. If you have any concerns during your stay, don't hesitate to communicate with the accommodation staff. Relax, explore the beauty of Alsace, and create cherished memories during your visit.

By following these steps, you can confidently book the perfect accommodation for your trip to Alsace. Consider your preferences, desired experiences, and budget when selecting your accommodation, and get ready to embark on an unforgettable journey through the breathtaking landscapes and rich cultural tapestry of Alsace.

8.5: Health, Safety & Emergency Contacts

Health

Medical Facilities & Insurance Coverage

Alsace boasts a reliable healthcare system with numerous medical facilities and hospitals. In case of a non-emergency medical issue, you can visit a local pharmacy ("pharmacie") where trained professionals can provide advice and over-the-counter medications. Make sure to carry comprehensive travel insurance that covers medical expenses, including emergency medical evacuation.

Vaccinations & Precautions

It is recommended to be up to date on routine vaccinations before you visit Alsace. Additionally, consider getting vaccinated against hepatitis A and B, as well as tick-borne encephalitis if you plan to explore rural areas. Tick-repellent and proper clothing (long sleeves, pants, and closed-toe shoes) are advisable when venturing into forested regions.

Drinking Water

Tap water in Alsace is generally safe to drink. However, if you prefer bottled water, it is widely available in supermarkets and convenience stores.

Safety

General Safety Precautions

Alsace is a relatively safe region, but it's always wise to take basic safety precautions. Keep an eye on your belongings, particularly in crowded areas and tourist sites. Don't flaunt your pricey items or bring about a lot of cash. Use reliable transportation options and be cautious when crossing roads.

Natural Hazards

Alsace is not prone to natural disasters; however, occasional flooding can occur along the Rhine River. Pay attention to weather forecasts and follow any instructions or warnings issued by local authorities.

Outdoor Activities

Alsace offers breathtaking natural landscapes, making it a perfect destination for outdoor activities. When engaging in hiking, cycling, or other recreational pursuits, ensure you are adequately prepared with suitable equipment, appropriate clothing, and navigation tools. Follow designated paths, adhere to any safety guidelines, and respect the environment.

Emergency Contacts

General Emergency Services

In case of an emergency, dial the European emergency number "112" to reach police, fire, or medical services. Operators are typically multilingual and will provide the necessary assistance.

Local Hospitals & Medical Services

If you require immediate medical attention, head to the nearest hospital ("hôpital") or medical clinic ("clinique"). Here are a few major healthcare facilities in Alsace:

- → Hôpital de Hautepierre (Strasbourg): +33 (0)3 88 12 74 00

- → Centre Hospitalier de Mulhouse: +33 (0)3 89 64 71 71

→ Hôpital Civil (Colmar): +33 (0)3 89 12 40 00

8.6: Local Customs & Etiquette

Greetings & Politeness

When meeting someone, it is customary to greet them with a handshake and maintain eye contact. Use "Bonjour" (good day) or "Bonsoir" (good evening) to greet people, and "Merci" (thank you) and "S'il vous plaît" (please) when interacting in shops, restaurants, or other establishments.

Dining Etiquette

When dining in Alsace, it's polite to wait until everyone is served before starting your meal. Keep your hands on the table and refrain from resting your elbows on it. It is customary to say "Bon appétit" (enjoy your meal) before eating. Remember to try local specialties such as choucroute (sauerkraut), flammekueche (tarte flambée), and the region's renowned wines.

Cultural Sensitivity

Respect the local customs and traditions of Alsace. When visiting religious sites, dress modestly and follow any guidelines posted at the entrance. Avoid discussing sensitive topics such as politics or religion unless you have established a close rapport with your conversation partner.

Language

While French is the official language in Alsace, you may encounter locals who also speak Alsatian, a Germanic dialect. Learning a few basic French phrases will be greatly appreciated, although many locals, especially in tourist areas, speak English.

By familiarizing yourself with the health, safety, emergency contacts, and local customs outlined in this guide, you'll be well-equipped to make the most of your visit. Remember to prioritize your well-being, respect the local customs, and embrace the unique experiences that await you in Alsace. Bon voyage!

Festivals & Events

Known for its picturesque canals, half-timbered houses, and rich cultural heritage, Colmar offers a delightful escape for travelers seeking a unique experience. In this guide, we will explore three remarkable festivals and events that showcase the vibrant traditions and warm hospitality of this enchanting town. From the renowned Colmar International Festival to the lively Fête de la Bière and the captivating Traditional Alsatian Celebrations, these events promise an unforgettable journey into the heart of Alsace's rich cultural tapestry.

9.1: Colmar International Festival

The Colmar International Festival is a world-class event that celebrates classical music, bringing together renowned musicians, orchestras, and music enthusiasts from all corners of the globe. Held annually, this festival provides an extraordinary opportunity to immerse yourself in the grandeur of classical compositions in Colmar's magnificent settings.

Highlights

The festival boasts an impressive lineup of concerts, recitals, and masterclasses, captivating audiences with exceptional performances. Renowned orchestras such as the London Symphony Orchestra, Berlin Philharmonic, and Vienna Symphony Orchestra grace the stage, creating an awe-inspiring atmosphere. The festival also showcases talented soloists, choirs, and chamber music ensembles, presenting a diverse range of musical genres and styles.

Venues

The festival utilizes Colmar's architectural gems as concert venues, adding a touch of enchantment to each performance. The Collegiate Church of Saint Martin, a stunning Gothic masterpiece, provides an ethereal setting for choral performances. The Unterlinden Museum, housed in a former convent, offers an intimate ambiance for chamber music recitals. Other venues include the Theater Colmar and the Eglise des Dominicains, ensuring a varied and immersive festival experience.

Extra Activities

Beyond the concerts, the festival offers educational workshops, lectures, and exhibitions, providing a deeper understanding of the music and its historical context. Visitors can engage with renowned musicians and gain insights into their craft through masterclasses and open rehearsals. The festival also organizes guided tours of Colmar's musical heritage, highlighting the city's close ties to renowned composers like Frédéric Chopin and Richard Wagner.

9.2: Fête de la Bière

Get ready to raise a glass at the Fête de la Bière, a lively celebration of beer, gastronomy, and conviviality. Taking place in the heart of Colmar, this annual beer festival invites locals and visitors alike to savor the rich brewing tradition of the Alsace region.

Beer Delights

The festival showcases a wide array of artisanal beers, ranging from traditional lagers and ales to unique seasonal brews. Local breweries, known for their craftsmanship and attention to detail, offer tastings that allow beer enthusiasts to explore the nuances of different flavors and styles. Accompanying the beers are delectable culinary delights, including Alsatian sausages, pretzels, and cheese, creating a perfect harmony of flavors.

Entertainment

Immerse yourself in the festive atmosphere as live bands, street performers, and traditional Alsatian dance troupes entertain the crowds. The lively music and spirited dance performances infuse the festival with energy and provide an authentic glimpse into the region's rich cultural heritage. Don't miss the famous barrel-racing competition, where teams compete in a thrilling display of agility and teamwork.

Family-Friendly Fun

The Fête de la Bière caters to visitors of all ages, ensuring a memorable experience for families. Children can enjoy a dedicated area with games, face painting, and interactive workshops that introduce them to the art of brewing in a fun and educational way. The festival also hosts a vibrant craft market, where local artisans showcase their creations, offering a chance to take home unique souvenirs.

9.3: Traditional Alsatian Celebrations

Immerse yourself in the rich cultural tapestry of the Alsace region by partaking in the Traditional Alsatian Celebrations. Throughout the year, Colmar hosts a series of festive events that pay homage to age-old customs, traditions, and folklore, offering an authentic glimpse into the local way of life.

Vineyard Festivals

Celebrate the annual grape harvest with lively vineyard festivals, known as "Fêtes des Vendanges." Witness the time-honored tradition of pressing grapes and enjoy wine tastings accompanied by traditional Alsatian music and dance. These festivals allow you to experience the vibrant spirit of the vineyards while savoring the renowned Alsace wines.

Carnival Festivities

Witness the joyous spirit of Alsatian carnival traditions during the Fasenacht season. Colorful parades, lively street performances, and elaborate costumes fill the streets of Colmar, creating a carnival atmosphere. Marvel at the intricately designed floats, join in the dancing and singing and indulge in traditional carnival treats like "Berawecka," a delicious fruitcake, and "Bretzels," a local pretzel specialty.

Easter Markets

During the Easter season, Colmar's charming squares and streets come alive with vibrant Easter markets. These markets showcase a variety of beautifully decorated Easter eggs, intricate crafts, and local delicacies. Visitors can immerse themselves in the festive atmosphere, participate in Easter egg painting workshops, and sample Alsatian Easter treats such as "Lammele" (lamb-shaped cakes) and "Coque de Pâques" (Easter bread).

Harvest Festivals

Apart from vineyard festivals, Colmar also hosts traditional harvest festivals in the surrounding countryside. These celebrations are an opportunity to witness the culmination of the agricultural cycle, where locals gather to express gratitude for a successful harvest. Visitors can experience traditional folk dances, participate in grape stomping, and indulge in seasonal culinary delights that highlight the bountiful produce of the region.

Alsatian Costume Parades

To truly immerse oneself in the cultural heritage of the Alsace region, attending an Alsatian costume parade is a must. These parades showcase the traditional attire of the region, with locals donning colorful traditional costumes, known as "trachten." The parades feature live music, dancing, and reenactments of historical events, providing a captivating spectacle that transports visitors back in time.

Saint Nicholas Day

Colmar embraces the tradition of Saint Nicholas Day, a beloved celebration that takes place on December 6th. Families gather as children eagerly await the arrival of Saint Nicholas, who is accompanied by his mischievous companion, the Père Fouettard. Saint Nicholas rewards good children with small gifts and sweets, while the Père Fouettard playfully threatens those who have been naughty. The streets come alive with processions, music, and festive decorations, creating a joyful and magical atmosphere for both locals and visitors.

Onion Market

The Onion Market, known as the "Ziwwelmaerik," is a traditional festival held annually in October. Dating back to the 17th century, this lively event pays homage to the humble onion, which was historically a staple crop in the region. The market features vendors selling onions in various sizes, shapes, and colors, as well as an array of onion-based products such as onion soup, onion tarts, and onion confit. Visitors can enjoy live music, and street performances, and immerse themselves in the vibrant atmosphere while savoring the unique flavors of the onion-inspired delicacies.

By partaking in these festivities, you will not only create lasting memories but also gain a deeper appreciation for the vibrant spirit and warm hospitality that defines Colmar and the Alsace region. So pack your bags and embark on an unforgettable journey into the heart of Colmar's extraordinary festivals and events.

ALSACE TRAVELS

Travel Tips & Recommendations

In this chapter, we will provide you with expert advice on the best time to visit, essential packing items, money-saving tips, itinerary, and other vital information to help you make the most of your journey. So let's start on this wonderful journey together!

10.1: Best Time to Visit Alsace

Alsace boasts distinct seasons, each with its allure. The region experiences a temperate climate, influenced by its proximity to the Vosges Mountains and the Rhine River. Choosing the right time to visit will greatly enhance your experience. Here are some seasonal highlights:

Spring

From April to June, Alsace blooms with vibrant colors as flowers blanket the landscape. The weather is pleasant, with mild temperatures ranging from 10 to 20 degrees Celsius (50 to 68 degrees Fahrenheit). Spring is the perfect time to explore the region's vineyards and witness the grapevines coming to life. Don't miss the opportunity to visit the charming villages during the Easter season when they are beautifully adorned with festive decorations.

Summer

Summers in Alsace are warm and inviting, with temperatures averaging between 20 and 30 degrees Celsius (68 and 86 degrees Fahrenheit). The region comes alive with various outdoor events, including lively street festivals and open-air concerts. Indulge in outdoor activities like hiking in the Vosges Mountains or cycling along the Rhine River. However, bear in mind that summer is also the busiest travel season, so plan on more people and more expensive accommodations.

Autumn

Alsace transforms into a picturesque wonderland during autumn, with the changing leaves creating a kaleidoscope of colors. From September to November, the weather gradually cools down, ranging from 10 to 20 degrees Celsius (50 to 68 degrees Fahrenheit). Explore the vineyards during the grape harvest season and participate in local wine festivals. Autumn is also an ideal time for nature lovers to embark on scenic hikes and capture stunning photographs.

Winter

Winter in Alsace is straight out of a fairytale, as snow blankets the villages and adds a magical touch to the region. From December to February, temperatures range

ALSACE TRAVELS

from -2 to 7 degrees Celsius (28 to 45 degrees Fahrenheit). Explore the enchanting Christmas markets in Strasbourg and Colmar, where you can savor traditional treats and shop for unique handicrafts. Winter sports enthusiasts can hit the slopes in the Vosges Mountains or enjoy ice skating in the outdoor rinks.

10.2: Packing Essentials

To ensure a comfortable and enjoyable trip to Alsace, it is essential to pack wisely. Here is a comprehensive list of items to consider:

Clothing

Pack clothes appropriate for the time of year you will be there. In spring and autumn, bring layers to accommodate temperature fluctuations. Summer requires light and breathable attire, including sunscreen and a hat. For winter, pack warm clothes, including a heavy coat, gloves, a scarf, and sturdy winter boots.

Comfortable Shoes

Alsace's cobblestone streets and picturesque villages are best explored on foot. Pack comfortable walking shoes or sneakers to ensure you can explore the region without discomfort.

Travel Adapters

Alsace operates on a European plug type (C and E). Bring a travel adaptor so you can charge your electronics.

Language Guidebook

While many locals in Alsace speak English, having a basic French language guidebook can be helpful, especially in smaller towns and villages.

Medications & First Aid Kit

Carry any necessary prescription medications, along with a basic first aid kit that includes items like pain relievers, band-aids, and antiseptic ointment.

Travel Insurance

Ensure you have travel insurance that covers medical emergencies, trip cancellations, and lost belongings. It provides peace of mind and protects you from unforeseen circumstances.

10.3: Money-Saving Tips

Traveling on a budget doesn't mean compromising on your experience in Alsace. Here are some helpful suggestions to assist you in saving money:

Accommodation

Consider staying in guesthouses, bed, and breakfasts, or vacation rentals instead of hotels. These choices can be more affordable and frequently offer a more genuine experience.

Transportation

Public transportation is efficient and affordable in Alsace. Utilize regional trains and buses to explore the area. Consider purchasing a transportation pass for unlimited travel within a specified period.

Dining

While Alsace offers a delectable culinary scene, eating out for every meal can be expensive. Explore local markets and grocery stores to buy fresh produce, cheese, and bread for picnics. Additionally, opt for lunch menus or "plat du jour" at restaurants for more affordable dining options.

Free Attractions

Alsace offers numerous free attractions that showcase its beauty and culture. Explore the charming villages, visit public parks, and wander through the picturesque vineyards without spending a dime. Take advantage of free guided walking tours offered in some cities.

Museum Passes

If you plan to visit multiple museums and attractions, consider purchasing a museum pass. These passes often provide discounted or free entry to popular sites, helping you save money while exploring the region's rich history and art.

Local Festivals & Events

Alsace hosts a variety of festivals and events throughout the year, many of which are free to attend. Experience the vibrant local culture by joining in these celebrations, which often feature live music, traditional dances, and local cuisine.

Shopping

When shopping for souvenirs, explore local markets and boutiques. Here, you'll find unique handmade crafts, locally produced wines, and traditional Alsace delicacies. Avoid touristy shops in popular tourist areas, as prices tend to be higher.

As you embark on your journey to Alsace, remember to plan your visit according to the seasons to make the most of the region's charm. Pack smartly, immerse yourself in the local culture, and utilize money-saving tips to ensure an unforgettable and budget-friendly adventure.

ALSACE TRAVELS

10.4: Itinerary

In this comprehensive 10-day itinerary, we invite you to discover the best of Alsace, immersing yourself in its rich heritage, savoring exquisite wines, and exploring picturesque towns along the way. Prepare yourself for a voyage that will enthrall and inspire you.

Day 1: Strasbourg - The Enchanting Capital

Begin your Alsace adventure in Strasbourg, the capital of the region. Spend your first day exploring the city's stunning historic center, known as Grande Île, a UNESCO World Heritage site. Marvel at the iconic Strasbourg Cathedral, a masterpiece of Gothic architecture, and take a stroll through La Petite France, a charming neighborhood characterized by its half-timbered houses and canals. Don't miss the opportunity to visit the European

Parliament, where you can gain insight into European politics. End your day with a delightful dinner at one of Strasbourg's renowned Alsatian restaurants, indulging in local specialties such as choucroute garnie (sauerkraut with sausages) and tarte flambée (Alsatian pizza).

Day 2: Colmar - A Fairytale Town

On day two, venture south to Colmar, a fairytale-like town renowned for its well-preserved medieval architecture. Lose yourself in the enchanting streets of the historic district, known as "Little Venice," characterized by its picturesque canals and colorful half-timbered houses. Visit the Unterlinden Museum, housed in a former convent, and admire its remarkable art collection, including the famous Isenheim Altarpiece. Immerse yourself in Alsatian culture by sampling local wines at one of the many wine bars, or enjoy a traditional Alsatian meal at a cozy restaurant. As evening falls, take a boat ride along the canals to experience Colmar's magical atmosphere under the glow of the city's lights.

Day 3: Riquewihr & Ribeauvillé - Medieval Gems

Embark on a journey to the medieval villages of Riquewihr and Ribeauvillé, nestled amidst rolling vineyards. Riquewihr, often regarded as one of the most beautiful villages in France, transports you back in time with its impeccably preserved half-timbered houses and charming cobblestone streets. Explore the village's boutiques and sample local wines at one of the many wineries. A short drive away lies Ribeauvillé, known for its three ancient castles that overlook the town. Wander through the narrow streets, admiring the colorful facades and soaking in the medieval ambiance. Don't forget to try a glass of Riesling, a signature wine of the region.

Day 4: Haut-Koenigsbourg Castle & the Wine Route

Today, discover the majestic Haut-Koenigsbourg Castle, perched atop a hill and offering panoramic views of the surrounding countryside. Step into the medieval world as you explore its fortified walls, towers, and interior chambers. Afterward, embark on a scenic drive along the Alsace Wine Route, a picturesque route that winds through vineyards, charming villages, and rolling hills. Make stops at various wineries along the way to sample Alsace's world-renowned wines, including Gewürztraminer, Pinot Gris, and Crémant d'Alsace. Take your time to savor the flavors and learn about the wine-making traditions directly from the passionate winemakers.

Day 5: Mulhouse & the Cité de l'Automobile

Head south to the vibrant city of Mulhouse, known for its industrial heritage and exceptional museums. Visit the Cité de l'Automobile, one of the world's largest automobile museums, housing a remarkable collection of vintage and luxury cars. Explore the captivating exhibits, including the iconic Bugatti collection, and delve into the history of automotive engineering. Afterward, wander through the historic city center, admiring its diverse architectural styles, and take a moment to relax in one of the pleasant parks. Mulhouse also offers an array of dining options, ranging from traditional Alsatian cuisine to international flavors.

Day 6: The Vosges Mountains & Outdoor Adventures

Escape to the natural beauty of the Vosges Mountains, a pristine landscape offering endless outdoor activities. Lace up your hiking boots and embark on a scenic hike through dense forests, discover picturesque waterfalls, or enjoy a leisurely picnic amidst nature's tranquility. During the winter months, the Vosges Mountains also offer excellent opportunities for skiing and snowboarding. If you prefer a more relaxed experience, take a scenic drive along the Route des Crêtes, a mountain road offering breathtaking panoramic views. Don't forget to savor the local mountain cuisine, including hearty dishes such as tarte aux myrtilles (blueberry tart) and Munster cheese.

Day 7: Obernai & Mont Sainte-Odile

Today, visit Obernai, a charming Alsatian town steeped in history. Explore its narrow streets lined with colorful buildings, visit the Market Square, and admire the beautiful fountain at the Place du Marché. Don't miss the opportunity to taste the town's famous gingerbread, known as pain d'épices. From Obernai, take a short drive to Mont

Sainte-Odile, a majestic mountain that is home to a revered pilgrimage site. Visit the Mont Sainte-Odile Monastery, perched atop the mountain, and enjoy the panoramic views of the Alsace plain. The monastery also houses a museum that provides insights into the region's religious history.

Day 8: Eguisheim & Wine Tasting

Eguisheim, a quaint village surrounded by vineyards, is your destination for today. Immerse yourself in its medieval charm as you wander through the concentric streets, marveling at the vibrant flower displays adorning the houses. Explore the village's castle ruins and the charming St. Leon Fountain. Eguisheim is renowned for its wine production, so take the opportunity to visit local wineries and indulge in tastings of the region's esteemed wines. Learn about the intricate process of winemaking and savor the exceptional flavors that make Alsace wines unique.

Day 9: Saint-Hippolyte & Kayaking on the River

Venture to the village of Saint-Hippolyte, nestled in the heart of the Alsatian vineyards. Discover its picturesque streets and visit the 16th-century Château du Haut-Kœnigsbourg, offering splendid views of the surrounding vineyards. In the afternoon, embark on a kayaking adventure on the tranquil River Ill. Drift along the water, surrounded by lush greenery and scenic landscapes. Whether you're a novice or an experienced paddler, kayaking provides a unique perspective of Alsace's natural beauty and allows you to appreciate the region's diverse flora and fauna.

Day 10: Return to Strasbourg & Departure

On your final day, return to Strasbourg and take the opportunity to explore any sights you may have missed during your first visit. Perhaps visit the renowned Strasbourg Museum of Modern and Contemporary Art or stroll along the picturesque Ponts Couverts. Enjoy a final meal at one of Strasbourg's charming restaurants, savoring the delectable Alsatian cuisine that has delighted your taste buds throughout your journey. As your adventure comes to an end, bid farewell to Alsace, filled with memories of enchanting towns, flavorful wines, and the warm hospitality of the region's inhabitants.

Each day of this 10-day itinerary has offered a unique and unforgettable experience, immersing you in the heart and soul of Alsace.

10.5: Shopping in Alsace

Strasbourg: A Shopper's Paradise

Start your shopping adventure in Strasbourg, the capital of Alsace. The historic city center is a treasure trove of boutiques, specialty stores, and high-end fashion brands. Head to Rue des Hallebardes for trendy fashion and accessories, or explore the charming shops along Rue des Grandes Arcades. Don't miss the famous Galeries Lafayette for luxury shopping and a wide selection of international brands.

Colmar: A Blend of Tradition & Modernity

Colmar is another must-visit destination for shopping enthusiasts. The city's cobblestone streets are lined with unique shops and boutiques, offering a mix of traditional Alsatian crafts and contemporary designs. Wander through the picturesque "Little Venice" district and discover local artisans selling pottery, jewelry, and handcrafted souvenirs. Rue des Clefs and Rue des Marchands are also worth exploring for their charming shops and galleries.

Mulhouse: A Hub for Textile & Design

If you have a penchant for textiles and design, Mulhouse is the place to be. The city has a rich industrial heritage and is famous for its textile production. Explore the bustling Rue du Sauvage, where you'll find a variety of fabric stores and ateliers specializing in unique designs. Don't forget to visit the Musée de l'Impression sur Étoffes (Museum of Printed Textiles) to learn about the region's textile history.

Riquewihr: A Quaint Shopping Experience

Nestled amidst vineyards and rolling hills, Riquewihr is a charming village that offers a unique shopping experience. Stroll along its narrow streets lined with half-timbered houses and boutique shops. Discover local products like Alsace wines, artisanal chocolates, and fragrant spices. Riquewihr is also known for its exquisite Christmas markets, where you can find handmade crafts and festive delights during the holiday season.

Markets & Fairs: Embrace the Local Flavors

Alsace is renowned for its vibrant markets and fairs, where you can immerse yourself in the local culture and find an array of regional products. Visit the Strasbourg Christmas Market, one of the oldest and most famous in Europe, to indulge in delicious treats, handcrafted decorations, and festive ambiance. Other notable markets include the Colmar Christmas Market, Mulhouse's Marché du Canal Couvert, and the Saturday Market in Obernai.

10.6: Traveling with Children & Pet

Family-Friendly Attractions

Alsace offers a wide range of attractions suitable for families with children. The Cité du Train in Mulhouse is the largest railway museum in Europe and guarantees an exciting journey through the history of trains. The Ecomusée d'Alsace in Ungersheim is an open-air museum where kids can experience rural life and participate in hands-on activities. For animal lovers, the Montagne des Singes (Monkey Mountain) and Parc de l'Orangerie in Strasbourg are great options.

Adventure Parks & Playgrounds

Let your little ones burn off some energy at one of Alsace's adventure parks or playgrounds. Europa Park, located near the border with Germany, is one of Europe's largest amusement parks and offers a plethora of rides and shows for all ages. The Cigoland theme park in Kintzheim is perfect for young children with its focus on storks and other local wildlife. Additionally, numerous public parks throughout the region provide playgrounds and green spaces for family picnics and relaxation.

Family-Friendly Dining

Finding family-friendly dining options is essential when traveling with children. Alsace is known for its delicious cuisine, and many restaurants cater to families. Look for establishments offering children's menus and high chairs. Traditional Alsatian dishes like tarte flambée (flammekueche) and spaetzle are often enjoyed by children as well. Some family-friendly restaurants to consider are Winstub La Hache à Foin in Strasbourg and Le Petit Pierre in Colmar.

Pet-Friendly Accommodation

When traveling with pets, it's important to find accommodation that welcomes furry companions. Many hotels, guesthouses, and vacation rentals in Alsace are pet-friendly, but it's always recommended to check in advance. Websites like Booking.com and Airbnb provide filters to search specifically for pet-friendly options. Remember to inquire about any additional fees or specific rules regarding pet stays.

Exploring Nature with Pets

Alsace boasts breathtaking natural landscapes, perfect for outdoor adventures with your pets. The Regional Natural Park of the Northern Vosges and the Alsace Wine Route offers scenic walking trails where you can enjoy the beauty of the region together. Some parks and gardens, such as the Parc de l'Orangerie in Strasbourg and the Parc de l'Orangerie in Colmar, allow leashed pets, providing a pleasant environment for a stroll.

Pet-Friendly Cafés & Restaurants

While pets are generally not allowed in restaurants and cafés, some establishments in Alsace make exceptions for well-behaved pets in outdoor seating areas. Look for places with designated pet-friendly zones or inquire with the staff before entering. Additionally, Alsace's wineries often have outdoor areas where you can enjoy tastings while keeping your pet by your side.

As you embark on your journey to Alsace, take advantage of the region's exceptional shopping opportunities and immerse yourself in its vibrant culture. Discover unique treasures in Strasbourg, Colmar, Mulhouse, and the picturesque village of Riquewihr. When traveling with children, explore family-friendly attractions, and adventure parks, and enjoy the delicious

ALSACE TRAVELS

Alsatian cuisine. If you're accompanied by your four-legged friend, find pet-friendly accommodation and explore the region's beautiful nature together. Alsace welcomes you with open arms and promises an unforgettable experience for every member of your family, be they human or furry. Bon voyage!

Conclusion

As you embark on your journey to Alsace, a region known for its rich history, picturesque landscapes, and charming villages, it's essential to have the right tools and resources at your fingertips. In this concluding part, we will explore the most useful mobile apps, online travel resources, and tourist information centers available to enhance your experience in Alsace.

11.1: Useful Mobile Apps

In this digital age, mobile apps have become indispensable travel companions. Here are some must-have apps that will enhance your visit to Alsace:

- ★ Alsace Wine Route (iOS, Android): Discover the renowned vineyards and wineries of Alsace with this app. It provides detailed information about wine producers, tasting notes, and events along the wine route.

- ★ Strasbourg Travel Guide (iOS, Android): If you're visiting the capital city of Alsace, this app is a valuable resource. It offers comprehensive guides, maps, and recommendations for exploring Strasbourg's top attractions, restaurants, and hidden gems.

- ★ Colmar Offline Map and Travel Guide (iOS, Android): Navigate the charming streets of Colmar with ease using this offline map. It includes information about popular landmarks, dining options, and local transportation.

★ Alsace Museums (iOS, Android): Immerse yourself in Alsace's rich cultural heritage through this app. It provides detailed descriptions of museums, exhibitions, and historical sites, helping you make the most of your visit.

★ Alsace Bike Trails (iOS, Android): Cycling enthusiasts will love this app, which offers a comprehensive guide to Alsace's bike trails. It includes route maps, difficulty levels, and points of interest along the way.

11.2: Online Travel Resources

A wealth of travel knowledge may be found online. Here are some online resources that will assist you in planning your trip to Alsace:

- ★ Alsace Tourism Website: The official website of Alsace Tourism provides a wealth of information about the region. From recommended itineraries to accommodation options, you'll find everything you need to plan your trip.

- ★ Alsace Wine Commission: For wine enthusiasts, this website is a valuable resource. It offers insights into Alsace's wine regions, grape varieties, and winemaking techniques. You can also find information about wine tours and tastings.

- ★ TripAdvisor: This popular travel website features user reviews, ratings, and recommendations for hotels, restaurants, and attractions in Alsace. It can be a helpful tool for finding hidden gems and avoiding tourist traps.

ALSACE TRAVELS

★ Rick Steves' Europe: Rick Steves' website includes comprehensive travel guides, podcasts, and videos about Alsace. His firsthand knowledge and expertise will provide you with valuable insights and tips for exploring the region.

★ Alsace Travel Blogs: There are several travel blogs dedicated to Alsace that offer personal experiences, itineraries, and insider tips. Some notable blogs include "Discovering Alsace" and "Alsace in a Glass".

11.3: Tourist Information Centers

When you arrive in Alsace, make sure to visit the local tourist information centers. They are excellent resources for maps, brochures, and personalized recommendations. Here are a few notable centers:

ALSACE TRAVELS

★ Strasbourg Tourist Office: Located in the heart of Strasbourg, this tourist office offers comprehensive information about the city's attractions, events, and public transportation. You can also book guided tours and purchase the Strasbourg Pass, which provides discounts and free entry to various sites.

★ Colmar Tourist Office: Situated in Colmar's old town, this tourist office is an excellent starting point for exploring the city. The staff can provide you with maps, itineraries, and suggestions for restaurants and activities.

★ Mulhouse Tourist Office: If you're visiting the city of Mulhouse, the tourist office here will provide you with all the necessary information.

They offer guided tours, maps, and assistance in multiple languages.

★ Riquewihr Tourist Office: Located in the charming village of Riquewihr, this tourist office specializes in providing information about the surrounding area. They can recommend wineries, hiking trails, and historical sites to explore.

★ Eguisheim Tourist Office: As one of the most beautiful villages in Alsace, Eguisheim has its own tourist office. Here, you can gather information about local attractions, bike rentals, and nearby vineyards.

11.4: Final Thoughts

Alsace is a region that captivates visitors with its unique blend of French and German influences, breathtaking landscapes, and vibrant cultural heritage. To make the most of your trip, utilize the various mobile apps mentioned in this guide, explore the wealth of information available online, and take advantage of the resources provided by tourist information centers.

Remember to immerse yourself in Alsace's rich history by visiting the numerous museums, exploring the enchanting villages along the Wine Route, and indulging in the region's world-renowned cuisine and wines. Be sure to check the local events calendar for festivals and cultural celebrations that will add a touch of magic to your experience.

Whether you're strolling through the cobbled streets of Strasbourg, admiring the half-timbered houses of Colmar, or savoring a glass of Riesling in a vineyard, Alsace promises a journey filled with unforgettable moments. Embrace the region's warm hospitality, savor its culinary delights, and let yourself be enchanted by the timeless beauty of Alsace.

Safe travels and bon voyage!

Printed in Great Britain
by Amazon